View from the Plaza towards the convent of Tepotzotlan

On the winding road from Mexico City to Puebla, between rows of long armed cactus, one of the numerous churches at Cholula suddenly appears like a dream castle in a fairy land.

DISCOVERING MEXICO

A Country In Transition

By
John A. O'Brien

The University Of Notre Dame

"I stood looking at it and thought that never, in the world would there be discovered other lands such as these."

Bernal Diaz, Companion of Cortes, On the Valley of Mexico, 1519

Printed in U. S. A.
July 26, 1943
By
OUR SUNDAY VISITOR PRESS
Huntington, Indiana

Nihil Obstat:
        REV. T. E. DILLON
                        Censor Librorum

Imprimatur:
    ✚ JOHN FRANCIS NOLL, D. D.
                    Bishop of Fort Wayne

To

Mr. and Mrs. Harry Wright

Who For Nearly Half a Century
Have Exemplified the Highest Ideals
Of American Life and Democracy to
Our Good Neighbors—the People of Mexico
The Author Dedicates This Work

TABLE OF CONTENTS

CHAPTER   PAGE

Chapter I

THE KEY TO UNDERSTANDING MEXICO

Mexico is a country of picturesque scenery, abounding in colorful contrasts, and embroidered with many a piece of Old World charm. The native Indians, whom one meets everywhere, carrying their packs, cooking their tortillas over charcoal fires, and selling spicy enchiladas, provide an atmosphere and a charming quaintness which intrigue and fascinate the visitor from the United States.

He quickly senses that this country, though adjacent to his own, is distinctly different. There are scenes strangely reminiscent of Europe and especially of Spain, but it is not a replica of the Old World. The omnipresent Indian with his handicraft civilization and his way of life give to the landscape a coloring which is missing from the European panorama.

In the capital the visitor sees buildings that range all the way from the fortress-like structures of the sixteenth century through the Baroque and Churrigueresque up to the very modern. Here he will find a flowering of art and culture which had its roots in the Old World.

A short distance away he will gaze upon the adobe hut of the Indian scratching a patch of mountain side and living much in the way his ancestors did in the days before the Conquest. Within a few minutes' ride from the capital he will see the artefacts of the three civilizations which preceded the arrival of Cortes and his soldiers, namely, the Archaic, Toltec and Aztec.

Throughout the Republic, in thriving cities, in the lonely countryside, and on picturesque mountain sites, he sees churches, monasteries and votive chapels. Many of these are splendid specimens of Old World architecture, and all of them cast a spell over the traveler, either because of their own architectural beauty or because of their picturesque setting. It is these stout-walled temples of God, many of them mellowed with the morning dews and the sunsets of the centuries, which give to the landscape its distinctive charm and makes it live for years in the memory.

Echoing Memories Of Spain

These quaint old churches, echoing with the memories of Spain, stand as the enduring monument of the courage, zeal and industry of those noble missionaries who left the culture of Aragon and Castile to plant among the natives of New Spain the faith of Christ. Theirs was a life of hardship and sacrifice. They had to contend with the rudeness and the barbaric customs of the Redmen of the forests and the mountains. Not infrequently did they have to struggle likewise against the cupidity of the *Conquistadores*. They blazed a trail of Christian civilization and culture through the Mexican wilderness from coast to coast, and left no tribe untouched by the saving truths of the Gospel of Christ. They were the true emancipators of the Indians of Mexico.

It has become the fashion among a certain school of writers on Mexico to exalt the primitive culture of the Indian tribes, to gloss over their barbaric customs and their savage cruelties, and to disparage the culture and the civilization brought by the Spaniards. This procedure does violence to the facts. The Indian tribes were not without a certain amount of architectural skill and culture, and their achievements are to be acknowledged with candor and pride. That recognition does not require, however, that the mighty civilization which the Spaniards brought to the Redmen is to be minimized or disparaged.

Neither does it mean that the mighty influence of the Church in lifting a polyglot nation of a hundred tribes from the dank darkness of paganism to the light and warmth of Christian life and culture is to be depreciated or ignored. The simple truth is that the greatest work ever done for the natives of Mexico was the work of the Spanish missionaries. It was a work of complete unselfishness in which the humble friars, Franciscan, Dominican and Recollect, gave all and asked nothing in return. They spoke to the untutored native of the forest with the convincing eloquence of their own example. They shared the hardships of the flock, and in humility and poverty of life imitated their divine Master who had not whereon to lay His head.

The Upraised Cross

Upon the ruins of pagan temples, where all too often human sacrifices were offered amid revolting rites to pagan deities, they reared the cross of Christ. That cross was to shine in the skies as the symbol of the reign of Christian faith and hope and love. Walk among the numerous churches at Cholula and you will find yourself wondering why there are so many in a settlement so small. Your wonder will persist and perhaps degenerate into unfounded criticism—as that of many an American

Looking up towards Cortes Palace from "down" town. Many of Cuernavaca's streets are too narrow for cars. Sure-footed little burros carry the loads.

tourist does—unless you take pains to discover the real cause. Then you will learn that this was the seat of an equally large number of pagan temples, and upon the ruins of each, the missionaries thought it well to erect a Christian church or chapel as an effective means of supplanting the savage cruelties of the pagan rites with the warmth, beauty and love of Christian life and worship.

The missionaries won the numerous pagan tribes to the Christian faith. They won likewise the respect and love of the Indians. That affection of the Indian for his *padre* exists down to the present day. In visiting among them in many different parts of the country, I found a deep attachment for their spiritual shepherd.

The persecution of the Church and the cruel treatment meted out to many priests was an affair instigated and executed by the *politicos*, hungry for the property of the Church. It did not spring from the natives, nor did it meet with their approval. But, as one who lingers long enough in Mexico will discover, the man who controls the army, controls the country. He need not consult the wishes of the inarticulate masses of the natives and he usually doesn't.

The Necessary Key

In spite of persecution, anti-religious laws, and oppressive measures launched by politicians with itching palms, Mexico is a Catholic country. Certainly more than 90 per cent are adherents. The non-Catholic writer, Hubert Herring, places the figure at 98 per cent. The visitor to Mexico will lack the key to the understanding of the country, and especially to the understanding of the life of the vast Indian population which constitutes the backbone of the country, if he fails to remember that fact. This is true, whether the visitor be a Protestant, Catholic, Jew or member of no faith.

Mexico is steeped in the Catholic faith. The history and traditions of that faith are reflected in the architecture, painting and sculpture of the people as well as in their social institutions. They are manifest in the interior decorations of the home, especially in the humble altar or votive candle burning before the picture of Our Lady of Guadalupe in nearly every Indian home, no matter how humble.

To the visitor who lacks that key, Mexico will remain a land of enigma, paradox and mystery. If he uses this key generously in his reading about Mexico or in his visits there, he will find many a door of Mexican life and culture opened to his understanding and insight.

Deepen Ties Of Friendship

In my sojourns in Mexico I came to know, admire and love its people. I mingled freely among all classes, among the Indians, the middle class and was privileged to meet many of its leading scholars, artists and writers. Incidentally I use the term Indian here and throughout the book to designate the person of dominantly Indian blood, with no thought of disparagement or no implication that he is not a Mexican. Like the Indian in our country who is the original, one hundred per cent American, the Indian there is a true one hundred percent Mexican. I always speak of him with respect. We in the United States will find upon acquaintance that we have much to admire in this great people and we have much to learn from them.

I have prepared these sketches—many were written on the spot—of some of the highlights of my travels south of the Rio Grande with a view of deepening the understanding, respect and friendship of the American people for their neighbors to the south. Friendship usually follows upon understanding. One of the important steps in promoting friendship between our two countries is to promote understanding and sympathetic understanding at that. I hope it will prove a contribution, however humble and modest, to the implementing of the Good Neighbor policy toward Mexico and all Latin America, upon which our nation has embarked with such good will and earnestness.

I hope this little book will prove helpful for the English speaking reader, whether Catholic or non-Catholic, whether he be a prospective visitor to Mexico or simply one who does his vagabonding by the more comfortable arm-chair method. I trust it may help the reader to discover the real Mexican. I send it on its errand of understanding and good will with the hope that it may not only afford interest to the reader but may serve to deepen the ties of friendship and affection between the people of America and our neighbors in Old Mexico.

Chapter II
A LAND OF CONTRASTS

Mexico is a Republic, composed of 27 states, the
Territory of Lower California and the Federal District. The form of its government, like that of the
United States of America, consists of three branches, the legislative, the executive and the judicial.
The Senate and the House of Deputies enact the
laws. The executive, as president, is charged with
their execution, while the courts, the supreme and
the lower ones, interpret them. In actual fact, the
president wields supreme power and virtually determines the national policy. He is the uncrowned
king.

The country is traversed by two great mountain
ranges, the one cutting across the eastern side is
called Sierra Madre and the one crossing the western, the Sierra Occidental. Between them lies the
great Central Plateau. As one travels through it,
he is impressed with the lack of water, of trees and
vegetation. It resembles a vast desert with various
kinds of cactus sprawling over the sandy soil. Here
and there we see little clusters of adobe huts and
wonder how humans can eke out a livelihood in so
inhospitable a soil.

80% Indian Blood

The population is estimated at twenty million.
About 80 per cent of the blood of the nation is Indian. The official language is Spanish, although vast
numbers of Indian tribes speak only their aboriginal
tongues. The great bulk of the Indian tribes live in
a backward, handicraft civilization, though some

individuals have forged to the front, commercially, politically and culturally. Thus the late Archbishop Diaz of Mexico City was of Indian blood.

Due to the great ethnograpical, economic and cultural differences of its inhabitants, Mexico is a land of striking contrasts. Here one finds all of the economic organizations and methods of trading known to mankind. They range from primitive methods of barter to the modern stock exchange. Here one finds primitive wooden plows scratching the surface along side of modern tractors; transportation on human backs and on burros as well as on trains and in airplanes

Here one sees the unbelievable poverty of an entire family living in an adobe hut of one room, while by its side rises a mansion of marvelous beauty. In short, the traveler can witness in a single day the entire gamut of social and economic history in any small region, even within the shadows of the Capital of the Republic.

Lack A Middle Class

Unlike the United States and most European countries, Mexico has lacked a middle class, wherein the strength of a nation lies. The population here has consisted chiefly of peons, peasants and laborers working for the most part for a mere pittance, and land owners and business men of great wealth. Since the bulk of the people are Indian with little or no education, they have been deceived times without number by false leaders who promised them heaven and earth in exchange for their support. Thousands of petty revolutions have swept across Mexico, leaving the leaders rich with booty and the followers poorer than before.

This scene shows Mexicans selling their
pottery in the Plaza. Note the burros which th
carrying their wares when not carrying the s
selves.

This scene shows Mexicans selling their home made pottery in the Plaza. Note the burros which they use for carrying their wares when not carrying the same themselves.

It is in the lack of a strong and influential middle class that the hub of Mexico's many difficulties lies. Since the population is widely scattered over mountain and valley, with little exchange of public sentiments between the denizens of the cities and the primitive scratchers of the soil in the mountain valleys, a strong and informed public opinion, as we have it in the States, seems to be largely lacking. The group in power formulate their own policies, with little hindrance from the vast Indian population scattered over the countryside.

An Indian Country

Without disparaging in the slightest the culture introduced by the Spaniards and still visible in every church, monastery, and chapel dating from the Colonial period, and with full acknowledgment of the European culture of some of the people in the cities, Mexico is still essentially a vast Indian country. The culture and social mores of the Indian are visible in every pueblo and countryside. While probably most of them speak Spanish, they still retain their patterns of agriculture, their primitive handicrafts and their essential mode of living.

Fundamentally religious, devoted to the Catholic Church, they constitute the backbone of Mexico's population and give the distinctive character to Mexico as a nation. So deep did the early Franciscan Friars place the faith in the heart of the Indian tribes, so indelibly did they write the story of their holiness upon the tablets of the Indians' memories, that almost a century of religious persecution has not been able to wean them from their Catholic faith.

Chapter III
LAREDO TO MEXICO CITY

Crossing the border of Laredo, Texas, we entered the colorful and picturesque land of Mexico. The International Highway from Laredo to Mexico City, is a splendid example of modern engineering. Having travelled over it the first week it was opened in 1936, we chose this time the Mexican National Railway.

It was past midnight when our baggage was inspected by customs' officers and the train started on its way. About three hours later we were suddenly awakened by a deafening noise and an enormous jolting that continued for several seconds. What could have happened?

Hurrying from our berth, we looked out to see trainmen scurrying with flashlights along the track. Our coach and the one next to it had inconsiderately left the tracks! Then we knew the meaning of the persistent jolting that made us wonder if we were crashing through a bridge.

No one was injured. The derailed coaches were left behind and the passengers moved into the other coaches until new ones could be secured at Monterrey. We thought ours was a novel experience—until we learned that this was not a rare occurrence on this road. There is a long stretch of road and it is difficult to keep it in good repair. But fortunately no one seems to be hurt from these derailings.

Spicy Enchiladas

At the various little towns at which the train stopped, Indian women and children carrying popular art objects and spicy enchiladas, hurried to the train windows. Food from uncovered dishes, and wrapped in newspapers was handed to the Mexican passengers—but not to the Americans.

Parallel to the railroad runs a range of mountains called Sierra Madre Oriental, that cuts across the Eastern region of the country. The country seems

Burros Still Popular In Mexico

The common mode of travel for Mexican families is still the burro. Here we see a typical family on the move, the husband in search of work and his wife and child with him. Their meager belongings are crated and packed on another burro. In the background as this picture was snapped were another father and his son who took turns riding the burro on their journey.

much like a desert with varieties of cactus and the maguey plant chiefly in evidence. Little adobe huts, baking under the sun, offered shelter to the Mexican Indians living along the railroad.

Abject poverty, such as seldom seen in the United States, characterized the appearance of the men, women and children who rushed out to meet the train whenever it stopped. Many of the men and women were barefooted, and their clothing approached the ragged stage. It was evident that the food, clothing and shelter which we have come to regard as the indispensable requisites for citizens in the States, were still strangers to our neighbors south of the Rio Grande. It is a land of contrasts and a country in transition. Old traditions are yielding to new modes of life which are coming for weal or for woe, from the friendly neighbor to the North.

Our first important stop on the road to Mexico City was at Monterrey. A progressive city with a population in the neighborhood of 150,000 and the capital of Nuevo Leon. It lies in the mountain valley of Santa Catarina Rio and is surrounded by picturesque country. It has an important steel industry and the largest brewery in Mexico.

The city was founded in 1596 by a Spaniard, Captain General Don Diego de Montemayor who solemnly named it "The Metropolitan City of Our Lady of Monterrey" in the name of the King of Spain. The Cathedral was begun in 1790 by Don Jose Rafael Verea, the second Bishop of Linares and took fifty years in the building.

The Bishop's Palace on Chepe Vera Hill was built in 1782 by the same prelate. The ancient chronicles relate that this was a year of famine and that the Bishop launched the building of the edifice to give employment to the many Indian victims of a terrible drought. Thus was anticipated many years ago one of the features of the New Deal.

First Printing Press

At the Red Reception room of the State Govern-

ment Palace may be seen an interesting relic of the
Colonial days in the form of the first printing press
brought to northern Mexico. It is interesting to note
that it was brought in 1813 by Padre Mier to print
the insurgent manifestos of the Mexican patriots.
The name of Father Mier belongs with the first
heroes of Mexican independence.

Among the other relics at this palace are the three
carabines used by the firing squad of Nuevo Leon
soldiers who shot the Emperor Maxmilian in 1867,
and thus brought to an end the ill-fated effort of
France to place a foreign ruler on the throne of
Mexico.

In Zaragoza Square in front of the Cathedral one
sees the plan that is followed throughout Mexico, as
it is throughout Spain, of having a great open space
where the people can assemble and build their social
and communal life around their common mother—
the Catholic Church. It is this pattern which gives
a singular beauty to innumerable towns and villages
which would otherwise be without distinction.

San Luis Potosi

After leaving Monterrey, we passed through a
number of picturesque towns and pueblos coming to
San Luis Potosi, the capital of the State of the same
name. The city has a population of more than
175,000 and is the center of a rich mining region.
The quaint old Cathedral is in the ornate Baroque
style, that was evidently so popular with the early
Spanish settlers. Even more interesting is the
Church of Nuestra Senora del Carmen with its tiled
dome and exceedingly ornate Baroque facade and
beautiful altars.

Upon our previous visit to Mexico in 1936, we

Wayside shrines are common along the Mexican countryside. Here is one before which a group of girls play as well as pray. Social and commercial life center around the churches of Mexico, as in Spain.

had the privilege of meeting the Ordinary of San
Luis Potosi, Bishop Guillermo Tritschler, one of the
most scholarly members of the Mexican hierarchy.
A former seminary professor, Bishop Tritschler has
exercised a wide influence upon the priests of the
Republic, many of whom studied under him. He is
likewise a noted archeologist.

Queretaro Historically Important

The next important stop was at Queretaro, the
capital of the State of the same name. Both architec-
turally and historically the city is important. It
contains some of the finest examples of Colonial
architecture, and it was here that the plans for
Mexico's independence were made.

On the Plaza de la Independencia stands the Municipal Palace, the former home of the Corregidora
Josefa Ortiz de Dominguez, one of the heroines of
Mexican Independence. On the second floor are a
number of portraits of benefactors of the city, and a
room in which Dona Josefa was a prisoner when she
sent the message to Father Hidalgo that his plans
for the freeing of Mexico from foreign rule had been
discovered.

On Santa Rosa street there stands El Convento
Colegiata de Santa Rosa de Vitervo, a 17th century
structure, remodelled by the famous architect,
sculptor and painter, Eduardo Tresguerras. Churrigueresque altars with unusually thick gold leaf dominate the interior.

The market place presents a colorful scene with
Indians bringing their products to sell. Many of
them are skilled in weaving, and sell their wares for
a pittance. The district was inhabited by Otomi Indians before the conquest and their inhabitants still

constitute the indigenous population of the city and
of the state.

A short distance from the city is the Cerro de Las
Campanas standing on a hill. A little chapel constructed by order of the Austrian government in
1901 marks the spot where the ill-fated Maximilian
and the two Mexican generals, Miramon and Mejia,
were executed. On Christmas eve in Queretaro there
takes place a unique and colorful celebration. The
Holy Family, angels and many of the Biblical char-
acters come in a solemn procession through the
streets, while the people sing and make merry.

Chapter IV
THE ROMANTIC STORY OF MEXICO CITY

After forty hours on the leisurely Mexican train, punctuated with many stops at little towns along the way, we were delighted when at last we pulled into the colorful and beautiful capital of the Republic, Mexico City. It lies in a mountain valley on the Central Plateau. As it is 7,440 ft. above sea level, the climate is surprisingly mild for a city so far south. The average temperature is 69 degrees F., the highest in the summer being 71 and the lowest in the winter 48. Its average of sunshine is said to be the highest of any of the large cities of the world. The rainy season extends from June to October, with rain occurring almost daily, usually in the late afternoon.

The capital now has a population of about a million and a half, having gained 500,000 since 1930. Mexico is thought to have been the name of one of the leaders of the Aztec group which founded the City of Tenochtitlan, now known as Mexico City. It was founded by a small band of nomadic Aztecs in 1325. It was constructed on a former lake, filled in over a long period of time. According to the ancient chronicles, the city resembled Venice with canals serving as streets. Why the Aztecs chose such a site for their city is shrouded in obscurity, but it is thought that the factor of defense from other warring tribes was uppermost in their minds.

From the city the mountains which surround it are visible. Constantly changing color from the play of cloud and sun upon them, they form a beautiful background for the ancient city of the Aztecs. Towering high up above the others in the Sierra Madre range are the two famous volcanoes. Ixtaccihuatl, meaning in Aztec, "White Woman," and Popocatepetl, signifying "The Mountain That Smokes."

These two snow-peaked mountains are shrouded in song, story and legend. Before the conquest, the

Scene At Xochimilco

Picture shows a flower-bedecked gondola moving along the canals at Xochimilco, fifteen miles south of Mexico City. Xochimilco is an Aztec word, meaning, place of flowers. It was the favorite playground of Aztec nobles and is still popular as a place of recreation and amusement. It is the Venice of Mexico.

Indians worshipped them as deities. On the days set aside for paying homage to them, there were enacted elaborate ceremonies, called Tepeylhuitl, or festival of the mountains. The Aztecs constructed a great wooden idol representing Ixtaccihuatl in their Great Temple, while of Popocatepetl they made a representation of a dough of amarand and maize seeds. To this day some Mexicans think they can discern the monumental body of a sleeping woman on top of Ixtaccihuatl.

Legend of the Aztecs

The following legend is told about the foundation of Mexico City six centuries ago—a legend that explains the symbols in Mexico's national emblem. While the Aztecs were looking for a site whereon to build their city, their chief priest had a vision in which their War God, Huitzilipochtli, told them to continue until they discovered an eagle on a cactus growing from a rock. The cactus would be the heart of his treacherous nephew, Copil, who had warred against him at Chapultepec.

For this act of insurrection, Copil was punished with death. Torn from his body, his heart was flung into the lake. It chanced to fall upon a rock among the reeds, and from it sprung up a large cactus upon which an eagle had built its nest. The War God ordered them to construct their temple on that very spot which would be the seat of their greatness.

At dawn one morning, their long search was rewarded. There before them was the eagle on the cactus! "His wings," says the ancient legend, "extended to the rays of the sun, taking color from it and from the morning freshness and in his claws a snake!" The Aztecs approached and reverenced the eagle as divine. This then is the quaint legend which explains the cactus and the eagle holding a snake in its beak upon Mexico's emblem.

The exact spot where the Aztecs constructed their first temple, presumably where the eagle was found, is shrouded in the mists of legend and uncertainty.

Chapter V
MEXICO'S CATHEDRAL: A LINK WITH THE PAST

On the north side of the principal plaza of the capital, above the ruins of the chief temple of the Aztecs, stands the Cathedral of Mexico City. Over the ruins of the Palace of Montezuma, on the east side of the plaza, rises the National Palace, the seat of the Government. The present Cathedral was begun in 1573, when the first one, erected in 1525, proved inadequate to meet the needs of the growing aristocracy. Dedicated to *La Asuncion de Maria Santisima,* the Cathedral was consecrated in 1667, though it was not completed till 1813.

When we pause to reflect that the first cathedral on this site was erected only 33 years after the epochal voyage of discovery by Christopher Columbus in 1492, we begin to realize how modern the great Cathedrals of our country are in comparison. The numerous churches, monasteries and schools which still dot the Mexican landscape tell in eloquent language the story of the zeal of the early Spanish missionaries to the land of the Mayas and the Aztecs.

The present Cathedral embodies the work of many architects and sculptors, and the century long toil of Indian laborers. The facade is Ionic, Doric and Corinthian, and the combination of gray stone with white marble in the decorations is arresting in its grandeur. There are two rows of Doric columns and a dome lofty and magnificent. Cruciform in shape, the edifice has fourteen chapels in the aisles on the side. Of these, the one which attracts much attention

from visitors is the first one to the right from the
main entrance, dedicated to the Father of Mexican
Independence, Father Hidalgo.

An Inspiring Vista

Rising to a height of 205 feet are the Cathedral
towers, visible from all parts of the city. The huge
bells, calling the people to prayer and to the Holy
Sacrifice of the Mass, are heard over a large area
of the capital which now sprawls out in every direction. The bell, Santa Maria, in the west tower
weighs 7,500 pounds.

The view from the towers affords an unsurpassed
panorama of city, valley and surrounding mountains. From this point of vantage, one perceives
more clearly than from the street, the numerous
churches with their swelling domes and uplifted
spires. Here he sees more plainly the profound influence of the religious motive in the building of this
ancient capital.

Here the visitor is able, especially in the late afternoon, to get the feel of the colonial city and to
appreciate its Spanish atmosphere and the religion
in which it grew up. In the vanishing light, with the
setting sun splashing the sky with crimson and gold,
the limits of the ancient city blend with the far off
horizons, and the new business edifices erected in
ultra-modern city style are softened by the twilight
as the peals of the evening Angelus summon the city
to prayer.

Protector Of Indians

While all classes attend the Cathedral, it is the
home chiefly of the poor. Bringing their children,
their food and sometimes even their dogs, the Mexican Indians make themselves at home in their

Father's house. They have the simple faith of children and a piety which finds expression both in prayer and in flowers which they place at the foot of the statues of Christ, the Blessed Virgin, and the Saints. In most of their churches, they display a fondness for covering their statues with robes, and thus seek

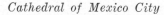

Cathedral of Mexico City

A close-up view of the majestic Cathedral of Mexico City. It is erected over the ruins of the chief temple of the Aztecs. The first edifice was built in 1525, and the present structure was begun in 1573 and completed in 1813. One of the noblest monuments in the Western Hemisphere, it has been the scene of some of the most important events in the history of the Mexican people.

to make them as realistic and as life-like as they can.

Leaving the Cathedral, my eyes fall upon an impressive statue of a Dominican friar. On the pedestal are inscribed the words: *Extranjero si amares la virtud, Detente y Venera—Este es Fray Bartolome de las Casas, Padre de los Indios.* "Stranger if you love virtue, pause and venerate. This is Fray Bartolome de las Casas, Father of the Indians." Such is the tribute which comes from the heart of the Indians of Mexico to the memory of this saintly missionary who was so fearless in protecting them from the covetous and exploiting hands of the Spanish conquerors.

It brought to my mind the magnificent painting in the *Palacio de Bellas Artes,* which portrays this brave friar standing at the door of a church to stay the cruel *conquistadores* in their efforts to seize and enslave the defenseless Indians. One of them is lying on the floor, clasping the feet of the friar, as her sole defense against the attackers. Thus did Fray Bartolome de las Casas reveal to the Indians the true spirit of that religion which he brought to them from across the seas. Thus too did Fray Bartolome carve for himself a niche in the history of the evangelization of Mexico and a niche in the hearts of the Mexican people who are overwhelmingly of Indian blood.

Center of Eucharistic Devotion

Across from Sanborns, the well-known American drug store and restaurant, is the historically important Church of San Francisco. Established in 1525 by the first twelve Franciscans who came to New Spain, the edifice was constructed largely from stones taken from the great Aztec Temple. For many years after the conquest, it was the chief center of religious instruction for the youth of the city. It was here that Fray Pedro de Gante, who established the first school for Indian boys in Texcoco, labored for many years. It was here that paint-

ing in the European tradition was first taught. Up
to 1860, practically every historical event in the
city was connected in some way with this church
and monastery. It is now in charge of the Society of
Jesus.

Adjoining San Francisco on the east is the Church
of San Felipe de Jesus. This is the church which
the Catholic visitor to Mexico will delight in visiting more frequently than all the others. For here
the Blessed Sacrament is exposed in a huge Osten-
sorium for adoration every day up till 9 o'clock at
night. The Church is kept immaculately clean and
placards request the faithful to abstain from too
audible praying or from any act which would dis-
turb the devotion of the adorers in the House of
God. Located in the heart of the business and shop-
ping district, Catholic tourists will find it easily
accessible for a visit to their Eucharistic Lord, for
confession, and for the hearing of Holy Mass, the
latest of which is said each day at noon.

The present edifice in unadorned Roman style,
dating from 1897, is dedicated to the Patron Saint
of Mexico City and the only Mexican canonized.
Born in Mexico in 1575, San Felipe de Jesus won
his crown of glory as a missionary in Japan. When
others, martyred in recent persecutions, are raised
in God's good time to our altars, Mexico will have
more than her share of canonized saints.

In the name of the thousands of Catholic visitors
to Mexico, the writer thanks the Church authorities
of the capital for the precious values afforded them
by this great center of Eucharistic devotion and
spiritual life. The Church is never without its quota
of worshippers, and some of my loveliest memories

of Mexico cluster about the Church of San Felipe de Jesus.

Palace Of Art

A short distance away stands the *Palacio de Bellas Artes* or Palace of Fine Arts, probably the most

Father Of The Indians

Painting in the Palace of Fine Arts in Mexico City, showing Fray Bartolome de las Casas. He is called the Father of the Indians.

impressive modern building in Mexico. Started by Diaz in 1900, and designed by the Italian Amado Bari, it was completed in 1934. The Mexican, Frederico Mariscal, whom the writer had the pleasure of meeting, was the architect for the interior. It is an ornate white marble structure with foreign and national elements and Maya motifs in the decorations of the main hall. It houses an elegantly furnished theater in which we heard the Mexican Symphony Orchestra under the direction of Chavez.

Visitors come here daily to view the collection of paintings, some of the best of which have come from Mexican churches. There is a fresco by Jose Clemente Orozco depicting in lurid colors the chaos of our present day world. On the opposite wall is a fresco by Diego Rivera on the theme: "Man at the Crossroads, Looking with Uncertainty but with Hope and High Vision to the Choosing of a Course Leading to a New and Better Future."

It is a glorification of Lenin and of the communist scheme of society. It satirizes the capitalistic order and depicts capitalists carousing with wine, women and song. I recognized the face of John D. Rockefeller, Sr., among the revellers with the arm of a harlot twined around his shoulder and a glass of champagne held in his hand.

Marx Or Christ?

The fact that Mr. Rockefeller was a teetotal abstainer, never engaged in carousing with women, wine or song, but was a model of domestic propriety and a devout Christian seemed to make no difference to Rivera. Like many Communists, he followed the practice of manufacturing facts to suit his thesis. As I looked at the grotesquely false portrayal of the character and habits of the dignified and sedate founder of the Standard Oil Company, it seemed to me that the satire was bouncing back upon the Soviet-minded painter making him look like a mountebank and a glorified purveyor of falsehood.

The fact that Rivera was able to use the wall

of this national edifice to glorify the atheistic materialism of Lenin, Trotsky and Stalin, throws a significant light upon the obsessions of previous administrations to fasten Soviet Communism upon a nation whose whole culture and traditions for the past four centuries have been rooted in the Christian faith. Not only art, but the schools as well, were pressed into service to uproot the Catholic religion of the overwhelming masses and to plant in its place the ideology of Marx with its scorn for religion.

During the regime of Cardenas, public school teachers were required to abjure their Catholic faith under penalty of dismissal and worse punishment. Calles, bloody and cruel, Cardenas, using not violence but the schools to uproot the Christian faith, have passed from power. The open doors of the Church of San Felipe de Jesus, scarcely a stone's throw distant, show that the Church in Mexico like the Church of the catacombs is triumphing over the powers of darkness because Christ is with her now, as He was in the first centuries, and as He shall be till time shall be no more.

Chapter VI
SHRINE OF GUADALUPE: THE LOURDES OF MEXICO

No tour of Mexico would be complete, if it did not include a visit to the most popular and the holiest of all its shrines—the shrine of Our Lady of Guadalupe. What the shrine at Lourdes is to France and to Europe, the shrine at Guadalupe is to Mexico and to all the Americas. Around that shrine are entwined, as garlands of flowers, the most touching expressions of the faith, piety and devotion of the Mexican people.

The numerous miracles wrought through the intercession of Our Lady of Guadalupe, and the numerous favors granted, as attested by acknowledgments in the shrine, show clearly that God has placed this people under the special patronage of His Blessed Mother. How efficacious is that protection is evidenced by the fact that repeated persecutions, combining both violence and subtlety, have made scarcely a dint in the deep and child-like faith of the masses of the natives.

The origin of this devotion is studded with miracles similar to those which brought into being three centuries later the cult at Lourdes. There the Blessed Virgin appeared in 1858 to a poor, fourteen-year-old girl, Bernadette Soubiroux, to make known her desire to have a shrine established there. As evidence of her apparition, Our Lady caused water suddenly to gush forth from the rocks—water which is flowing to this day. The vast number of crutches, wheelchairs, and other signs of invalidism which

have been left there by suddenly cured cripples have
made known to the world the efficacy of Mary's intercession.   Even non-Catholics have taken cog-
nizance of this monumental evidence, and Franz
Werfel's *Song of Bernadette* has become a classic,
carrying to those of every faith the amazing story
of Lourdes.

Apparition Of The Virgin

The story of Guadalupe begins on Saturday, December 9, 1531, when the Blessed Virgin appeared
to the fifty-five year old Indian, Juan Diego, as he
was hurrying down Tepeyac hill to hear Mass in
Mexico City, about three miles distant. Addressing
him in sweet and tender tones, and calling him "my
son," Our Lady asked him to be her messenger to
Bishop Zumarraga and to tell him that she wished
a shrine built on that spot from which she would
watch over and love his people. It is to be noted
that the place where the Virgin appeared was the
site of an old Aztec temple, in which Tonantzin, the
Aztec goddess of the Earth and Corn had a wide cult.

Much bewildered, Juan obeyed. After considerable difficulty, he obtained an interview. The bishop,
however, was sceptical. On the following day, Sunday, the Virgin again appeared to Juan, who told
her of the bishop's doubts and asked her to send a
worthier messenger. Insisting, however, that she
had a reason for her choice, Our Lady directed him
to go again to the bishop. Still doubtful, the bishop
bade him bring a sign from the lady who said she
was the mother of God.

All day Monday, Juan was busy, caring for an
uncle, Bernardino, who seemed dying of fever. So
at dawn on Tuesday, December 12, Juan was run-

CAPILLA DE LA IGLESIA DE GUADALUPE MEXICO.

On the main altar of the Shrine is the miraculous
picture of Our Lady of Guadalupe which is the center
of Mexican devotion. The picture has withstood in
seemingly miraculous manner all efforts to destroy it.

ning to St. James's convent for a priest. Seeking to avoid the apparition and fearing a scolding, Juan took a different path, going round where the well chapel now stands. But Juan did not escape.

"What Road Is This ... ?"

Crossing down to meet him, the Blessed Virgin asked:

"What road is this thou takest, son?"

A tender dialogue followed. She reassured Juan about his uncle, whom at that instant she cured, appearing to him likewise and calling herself Holy Mary of Guadalupe. She bade Juan go again to the bishop.

Whereupon Juan asked for a sign. She directed him to go to the top of the hill and gather roses. Knowing that it was neither the time nor the place for roses, Juan nevertheless obeyed. To his surprise and delight, he found a profusion of roses which had sprung up from the barren rocks. Placing many in the lap of his *tilma,* a long cloak worn by Mexican Indians, Juan returned. Rearranging the roses, the Blessed Mother instructed him to keep the roses untouched and unseen till he delivered them to the bishop.

When he was again received by the bishop, Juan unfolded his cloak and the roses fell out. But he was startled to see the bishop and his attendants kneeling before him, until he looked where their eyes were riveted. Lo and behold! There upon his poor *tilma* was glowing the figure of the Virgin Mother just as she had appeared to him.

The picture immediately became the object of great veneration. It was carefully guarded in the bishop's chapel, and later was borne in solemn procession to the preliminary shrine.

A Miraculous Picture

The picture and the material upon which it appears have been the objects of prolonged scrutiny and investigation. The material is coarsely woven, and is as thin and open as poor sacking. It is made of vegetable fibre, apparently from the *maguey* plant, which abounds in Mexico. It is composed of two strips about seventy inches long and eighteen wide, held together by weak stitching. I could make out the seam running up the middle of the figure, and turning aside from the face.

How the colors were laid on such material passes the understanding of painters. They have testified that the "canvas" was not only unfit, but unprepared. The flowerlike tints and the abundant gold provoke their admiration, while the apparent oil, water, distemper, etc. coloring in the same figure causes them to marvel. Artists are unanimous in proclaiming the proportions perfect for a young maiden. The figure of the virgin with the sun, moon and star accompaniments of the great apocalyptic sign, along with the supporting angel under the crescent, is taken as representing the Immaculate Conception.

Moving with her customary caution and prudence, the Church subjected all the occurrences at Guadalupe to careful study and investigation. At numerous hearings sworn evidence from many sources corroborated the traditional account of the miraculous origin and influence of the picture. Vouchers were produced for the existence of the letter of Bishop Zumarraga to his Franciscan breth-

The well known and dearly beloved Lady of Guadalupe is shown upon a background typifying Southwestern America together with Mexico and Central America as well. "Her Grace of Guadalupe" shines resplendent while the ancient Mayan and Aztec sacrificial altars stand deserted, the prey of an encroaching jungle.

ren in Spain. The historian, Bernal Diaz, a companion of Cortez, in 1568 refers incidentally to Guadalupe and its daily miracles. For more than four centuries the clergy, secular and regular, and especially the bishops have been unwavering in their devotion.

Papal Approval

Benedict XIV decreed that Our Lady of Guadalupe should be the national patroness and made December 12, a holyday of obligation. Leo XIII ordered the picture to be crowned in his name. In addition to permitting Mexican priests to say the Mass of Holy Mary of Guadalupe on the twelfth day of every month, Pius V granted indulgences which may be gained in any part of the world for prayers said before a copy of the picture.

In 1532 a shrine was constructed at the foot of Tepeyac hill and served for ninety years. It is still standing, forming a part of the parochial sacristy. In 1622 a larger shrine was erected, and in 1709 there rose a still more imposing one. Aggregated to St. John Lateran in 1754, it was created a basilica in 1904. In recent years the shrine has undergone a complete interior renovation in gorgeous Byzantine with beautiful murals portraying the story of Guadalupe.

The writer was privileged to say Mass at the main altar of the shrine and to stand so close that the acid stain, caused by a vandal who sought to destroy the picture, was clearly visible on the side.

There was nothing to indicate, however, that the picture had been affected in the slightest way. Professor J. E. Vera, formerly of Notre Dame University was to serve my Mass, but when he was un-

able to come, three of his students, Edward Paredes,
Alejandro Armendariz and Paschal Ortiz Rubio, son
of the former President of Mexico, took his place.
All three are now students at Notre Dame.

Unscathed By Bomb

I saw the crucifix and the metal candlesticks
that were twisted out of shape by the explosion of
the bomb hidden on the altar below the painting of
the Virgin. To destroy this centre of Catholic devotion has long been the object of the enemies of the
Church. But while the bomb spent its fury on the
altar, blasting huge pieces out of the marble, and
hurling debris in all directions, the miraculous picture remained unscathed. Thus did Almighty God
demonstrate the protection with which the image
of His Blessed Mother is shielded and manifest His
approval of the singular devotion to Our Lady of
Guadalupe.

During the persecution of the Church under
Calles, plans were made to destroy the famed picture. Word leaked out. The next morning there
was such a vast concourse of men, women and children surrounding the shrine, that the soldiers departed without molesting the church and its precious
treasure. The speed with which the faithful went
from house to house, and the mighty hosts of people
who responded to the appeal and showed themselves
willing to die, if necessary, in defense of their Blessed
Mother and the likeness miraculously vouchsafed to
them, disclosed more clearly than many volumes the
depth of their devotion and loyalty to Guadalupe.

Faith Incarnate

On all the days on which I visted the shrine
there was a constant stream of pilgrims coming from

all parts of the Republic, and some coming from the
countries of Central and South America. Some of
the natives were wearing the colorful costumes distinctive of their respective regions. Among the
pilgrims I noticed a Chinese father and his two
daughters.

From the ninth to the twelfth of December, in-
clusive, huge throngs of pilgrims march to the
shrine, some of them walking for days and for weeks.
The shrine, the streets and the nearby hills become
so full of pilgrims, who eat and sleep out of doors,
that there is scarcely room to move.

Carrying a lighted candle or a bouquet in their
hand, they move on their knees down the center
aisle from the door to the altar rail. I can still see
the face of one Indian as he moved slowly along on
his knees. The light burning in his deep-set eager
eyes, lighting up his swarthy countenance, matched
the lighted candle which he carried in his right hand.
In that silent figure I saw a product of the faith,
planted in the heart of the Mexican Indians by the
zeal of the early missionaries, which the storms
and vicissitudes of four centuries have not been able
to mutilate or destroy. He was a picture of faith
incarnate, of the faith that moves mountains, and
of the faith that fain would summon a warring
world to make its peace at the feet of the Blessed
Mother of God.

Chapter VII
CHURCH ATOP PYRAMID

It is the fashion in certain quarters to exalt the culture of the early Indian population of Mexico and to disparage the cultural contribution of the Spaniards. Some writers are fond of depicting the Aztecs, Toltecs and Mayas as possessors of a civilization superior to the Christian culture which the Spaniards brought to the land they called New Spain. This fanfare is part of the technique used by those who are pagan at heart to glorify the license of paganism and to decry the restrictions imposed upon the passions by the so-called "corseted" civilization of Christianity.

If any reader has come under the spell of that mood and wishes to get a dash of the cold water of disillusioning reality thrown in his face, let him ride out 28 miles from the capital to the pyramids at San Juan Teotihuacan. There he will see the Pyramid of the Sun and the Pyramid of the Moon. For the sun and the moon were worshipped as gods under the names, Tonatiuh and Metzli. Towering above these nature gods, however, was the war god, Huitzilipochtli, the real head of the Aztec pantheon.

Highway Of The Dead

These two huge adobe pyramids rise up to impressive heights while their bulk makes one wonder how the Toltecs were able to construct with their primitive tools such large edifices. They carried my mind back to the time when I stood in wonder and awe before the still more impressive pyramid at Gizeh, a few miles outside of Cairo, Egypt.

The Pyramid of the Sun is 260 feet high, while its base covers a surface of about 130,000 square feet. The construction is divided into five pyramidal terraces, and on the western side, a large wide stairway leads to the top. The Pyramid of the Moon is smaller, rising 165 feet and covering at its base about 53,000 square feet. A highway leading to the pyramids is known at *La Via de los Muertos,* the Highway of the Dead.

Thousands Of Human Victims

The name is significant. For over this highway the Toltecs would lead the thousands of cap-

Church Atop Cholula Pyramid

The Church of the Virgin of Los Remedios stands atop Pyramid at Cholula and symbolizes the triumph of the Christian religion over the blood-thirsty paganism of the Toltecs. It is one of the most arresting scenes in Mexico.

tives, taken in their interminable wars, as sacrificial victims, to their blood-thirsty god. When the victim would reach the top, where stood an altar, the Toltec priest would slash open the breast with his obsidian knife, tear out the heart still throbbing, and hold it up as the favorite delicacy to appease his bloody Moloch.

Down below would be the captor and his friends waiting for the carcas to be tumbled down the steps for them to carry home to be cooked for the feast of victory. On some days several thousand human victims would be slaughtered in this manner so that the sides of the pyramid would be covered with a stream of blood.

While the cries of the victims assailed the ears and the stench of human slaughter filled the nostrils, the Toltecs rejoiced in being able to offer so many throbbing human hearts to their fiendish deity. Here is the true picture of the culture of the Aztecs and Toltecs. Herein is mirrored the most blood thirsty religion which the world has even seen. This is the religion, reeking with the stench of human sacrifice, which the Spaniards replaced with the religion of the gentle Christ.

Babies Sacrificed To False Gods

As I stood on the summit of the Pyramid of the Sun and looked out into the distance, I could see with my mind's eye the long procession of human victims being led by the Toltec captors like sheep to the slaughter. Try as I could, I was unable to recall anything in the history of the pagan world where human cruelty and butchery were practised in the name of religion on so large and so systematic a scale.

The calendar of religious festivals for the Mexican year has been preserved. In each 20-day period we find one or more festivals calling for acts of human torture, including the passing of sharp sticks through the tongue.

The rain gods or Tlalocs were propitiated during the month of the "diminishing of water" by a procession of Toltec priests with music of flutes and trumpets, carrying on plumed litters infants with painted faces, in gay clothing with colored paper wings, to be slaughtered on the mountains or in a whirlpool in the lake. So cruel and bloodthirsty was their religion that it had quenched all human sympathy, which alone explains how they could delight in the torture of the most helpless of all creatures— little babes.

Church For Every Day Of The Year

After viewing the pyramids at San Juan Teotihuacan, I traveled over the highway to Puebla. Some seven miles before reaching Puebla, the road skirts Cholula, the ancient city of the Toltecs. While now but a small town, it was once a populous Indian center. For its size, it has the largest number of churches of any city in the world. The guides and the guide books almost without exception tell the visitor that it has a church for every day in the year. The most that Professor J. E. Vera, former secretary of Archbishop Vera of Puebla, and I could count were about forty.

As the traveler nears the town, a pyramid looms up before him. On its summit stood in centuries past the hemispherical temple of Quetzalcoatl. But upon the ruins of the pagan temple there rises now a Christian church, dedicated to the Virgin of *Los*

Remedios. Surmounting its pinnacle was the Cross of Christ, reaching high into the skies of Mexico to proclaim to its inhabitants and to all the world the victory of the religion of Christ over the bloodthirsty paganism of the Toltecs.

It was an arresting picture and I asked our driver to stop the car that we might make a pilgrimage to the top. As we started to climb the pyramid, a guide offered to take us into the tunnels which the Government has made into the interior. We followed him for what seemed like a well-nigh inter-

The Pyramid of the Sun

The Pyramid of the Sun at San Juan Teotihuacan about twenty-eight miles from the capital is one of the most impressive monuments that has survived from Mexico's past. Larger in mass than the great pyramid of Egypt, it was the scene of indescribable bloody sacrifices to Toltec gods—more than a thousand human victims being sacrificed at the altar on its summit in a single day.

minable groping in the darkness, till finally the guide
paused and said: "Here we are in the center of the
pyramid, directly below the stone upon which the
sacrificial human victims were slaughtered."

After another long groping, we emerged from
the darkness into the light of the exterior and resumed our climb. On the summit we entered the
lovely little church of the Virgin. A group of men,
wearing the large scapulars of sodalists, were reciting the rosary. We bowed our heads in prayer before the tabernacle of the Eucharistic King, and
then joined our Mexican brethren in paying homage
to the Mother of God.

Seemed Like A Dream Come True

It seemed almost like a dream come true. Here
we were in the place that once marked the greatest
concentration of temples to the monstrous gods of
the pagan Toltecs. Upon the ruins of everyone
of them, zealous missionaries of Christ, sons of St.
Francis, had erected a church to the true God. Hence
the large number of churches which now mystify
and amaze the visitor.

Here we were kneeling in the church which
arose upon the ruins of the Toltec temple which once
stood on the loftiest eminence as the symbol of
the reign of pagan idolatry throughout the land.
Here was a church whose location, more picturesque
than any I could recall in Europe or in America,
symbolized the victory of light over darkness, of
gentleness over brutality, of love over hatred, of
Christ over Quetzalcoatl and all the other bloody
deities of Toltec paganism.

Humbly, reverently, with hearts bursting with
joy and gladness, we thanked God for those daunt-

less soldiers of Christ who left the peace and se-
curity of their Spanish homeland to brave the perils
of the sea, the perils of the wilderness, the perils of
martyrdom, to bring to the savage Redmen in the
New World the priceless blessings and the precious
heritage of the faith of Christ.

Seldom, if ever, did I find it so difficult to drag
myself away from a Church. At last we arose and
turned from the candle-lit altar, with the image of
the *Virgin de los Remedios* smiling down upon us,
and departed. Darkness was already wrapping the
landscape with its somber pall. Storm clouds were
gathering overhead. Soon rain began to fall.

At the foot of the pyramid, I turned for one last
lingering look. A light was shining now from the
cross pinnacled on the church's spire. The symbol
now was perfect. Christ, the Light of the World,
was reigning in the tabernacled altar on Cholula's
tallest pyramid—the same Christ that will reign
forever in the hearts of the Mexican people.

Chapter VIII
CATHOLIC ACTION IN MEXICO

What about Catholic Action in Mexico? Is there much evidence of the activities of the Lay Apostolate? Are the Catholic people instructed and organized to be able to resist the flood of Protestant propaganda now being released upon them? Will they hold fast to the priceless heritage of the Faith of Christ in spite of the army of Protestant missionaries, no longer able to work in the Orient, who are now directing their footsteps to the Republic south of the Rio Grande?

These are questions in the minds of many Catholics in the United States today. They were not absent from my mind as I traveled through Mexico and talked with priests, bishops and lay people in all walks of life.

The American tourist who passes a week or two in Mexico, visits a few of the historic churches in the capital, and thinks of them largely as empty shells of a dead past, does not catch even a glimmering of the Catholic lay activity going quietly on behind the scenes. Let such a person get out of his car at 137 Edison St. in the capital and he will see an institution truly unique—*Feminina Cultura.*

Unique Institution Does God's Work

Here the great leader of Catholic Action among the women in Mexico, Miss Sofia del Valle, has established a school for the training of girls to serve as catechists throughout the Republic. Because nuns were driven out of the country, their schools closed, their properties confiscated by the persecutions of

Calles and Cardenas, there has been for the past decade a serious dearth of religious to instruct the children in the teachings of their holy faith. In consequence many thousands have been growing up with no systematic religious instruction.

To meet that urgent need, Miss del Valle has organized a training center in which young women are thoroughly grounded in the philosophy and religion of the Catholic Church. The faculty, which is drawn largely from priests teaching at the seminary now functioning on the outskirts of the capital, offers courses extending over a four year period. The instructors seek to train the girls, ranging from eighteen to twenty-five years of age, not only in the exposition of the great dogmas of the Catholic faith, but in answering objections which are now being scattered among the people by Protestant missionaries.

I visited the school, audited some of the classes, and spoke briefly to the student body. The sight brought back to my mind that other noble expression of the lay apostolate, the work of the Catholic Evidence Guild in London. A dozen years ago in St. Peter's Guild Hall in the basement of the Westminster Cathedral in Britain's teeming metropolis, I had seen young men and women being trained under the experienced eyes of Francis J. Sheed and his wife, Maisie Ward Sheed, to preach the truths of the Catholic faith to the great motley crowds in Hyde Park and to withstand the heckling which usually greeted them.

More Than 100,000 Are Instructed

Here was a kindred movement. Differing in methods and in points of emphasis, because of dif-

ferences in the two countries, the two movements
sprang from the same deep Catholic instinct—the
instinct to pass on their precious heritage of divine
truth to their fellow countrymen as well as to their
kindred. It shows that when the need arises, the
zeal of the laity will find a way to express itself, so
that Christ's injunction to teach all nations the im-
perishable truths of eternal life, shall forever be
fulfilled.

"More than 100,000 children and adults," said
Miss del Valle, "are now being taught the catechism
as well as advanced courses in religion through these
catechists who are now ministering in every diocese
of our country. Many bishops have written in to
say that the work of these catechists is bringing
instruction to children who could never otherwise
be properly prepared for First Holy Communion, to
say nothing of being trained to refute attacks upon
their faith."

How Support This Work?

"How do you support this work?" I asked.

Miss del Valle smiled. "It isn't easy," she said.
"But poor as most of our people are, they give generously. Then whenever I can spare the time, I go
to the United States and give a few lectures on our
work and return with additional funds.

"Your countrymen have been generous in helping us carry on," she continued, "and I would like
them to know how much we appreciate it."

That afternoon I visited the offices wherein she
and her assistants carried on extensive correspond-
ence, giving additional guidance and direction to
their graduates, many of whom are carrying on

their ministry in isolated mountainous regions, with little opportunity to receive the counsel of pastors.

"First Woman Of Mexico"

A member of a distinguished Catholic family, with an education received in the best schools of Europe, Miss del Valle has rendered a service to the Church that merits for her the title "The First Catholic Woman of Mexico." Wearing the garb of a lay woman, she is doing the work of a consecrated nun. What Miss Pilar de Rivera is doing through the *Auxilio Social* for the needy of Spain, what Mrs. Maisie Ward Sheed is doing through the Catholic Evidence Guild for the dissemination of Catholic truth in England, Miss Sophia de Valle is doing through her trained social workers and catechists for the poor and needy and the unchurched people and children of Mexico.

"Father," she said, as I was leaving, "don't forget Bishop M. D. Miranda. He has been a pioneer in the Youth movement in Mexico, and we are all in debt to him for his vision, zeal and courage."

We Introduce Father Castiello

What about the work for the Catholic young men in Mexico?

I went over to its headquarters at 120 Avenida Hidalgo in the capital, and met Father Alfonso Castiello, S.J., the Director of Catholic Action among the young men of Mexico. The meeting stirred memories. In 1937, his brother, Father Jaime Castiello, S.J., had spent nearly a week with me, when I was chaplain at the University of Illinois. While I have been among University professors for more than thirty years, I rate Fr. Jaime Castiello, S.J., as one of the most gifted scholars it has been

my lot to know—sharing the triumvirate with Dr.
Alexis Carrel and Prof. Robert Andrews Millikan.

On his way back to Mexico after spending fifteen years in the best universities of Europe and
America, speaking seven languages fluently, Fr.
Jaime Castiello, S.J., hoped to spend himself in working for the youth of Mexico. In the few months he
labored there, he captured the imagination and fired
the zeal of the University students in the capital. His
tragic death in an automobile accident robbed the
Church of Mexico of one of its most brilliant scholars
and promising apostles. His memory, however, and
the flame of the missionary crusade he kindled,
linger on.

Similarly gifted in talent and ripe European
culture, Father Alfonso Castiello, S.J., is building
up a mighty organization of the young men of the
Republic, and is directing its manifold apostolate in
combating Communism, religious indifferentism,
and in giving to the Church in Mexico what it so
sorely needs—a trained and efficient body of lay-
men to weave the saving truths of the Catholic
religion into the social, economic and public life of
the nation.

"Give Me A Lever Long Enough . . ."

"Give me a lever long enough," cried the ancient
Greek physicist, Archimedes, "and I will move the
earth." The lever which Father Alfonso Castiello is
seeking to fashion is the lever of a highly trained and
efficiently organized lay apostolate which will translate Christ's law of justice and mercy and love into
the private and public life of the nation.

Among many others helping Father Castiello
to attain his great objective are Fathers Gabriel

Notre Dame Alumni In Mexico

University of Notre Dame Alumni and their wives turn out for the first meeting of the newly organized Notre Dame Club of Mexico. The club was organized by Father John A. O'Brien, University of Notre Dame professor, to assist the lay Apostolate in Catholic Action and to promote closer ties of culture and friendship between Mexico and the United States.

"Every Notre Dame alumnus," said Mr. Edward Trueblood of the American Embassy, "will be a goodwill ambassador, interpreting to the people of Mexico the ideals of freedom and democracy for which the United States is pouring out her blood and her treasure in all the countries of the world today." In the second row, from left to right are: Prof. Paul V. Murray, Principal of the American School, Rev. John A. O'Brien, Ph.D., Father Alfonso Castiello, S.J., Director of the Youth Organization of Mexico, and Harry Newning, alumnus of the class of 1915.

Mendez Plancarte with his able monthly journal, *Abside,* and Angel Maria Garibay with his scholarly lectures on Thomistic philosophy to the young men of the capital.

Mention should likewise be made of the magnificent work of Prof. Paul Murray, principal of the American High School, whose able leadership in education is enhancing the esteem of the Mexican people for both the Church and the United States. I found him both admired and loved by the young people of the capital, many of whom had studied at his school.

Notre Dame Club Formed In Mexico

With a view of assisting Fr. Castiello in a humble way, I organized a Club of the Notre Dame Alumni living in the Federal District. Several hundred Mexican students have been educated at Notre Dame and many of them are living in the capital and in its suburbs. Among the prominent alumni of Notre Dame was Eduardo Hay, recently deceased, who at one time was Secretary of State. Others are rapidly forging to positions of leadership in the business, professional and cultural life of the Republic.

With the help of alumni Harry Newning and L. J. Urbanek, coach at the American school, and of Rafael Alducin, a senior at Notre Dame, I got a good turn-out of old students at a dinner meeting at the American Club in Mexico City. Many of the old-timers had not seen one another for years. Songs of the University were sung, and the spirit, for which Notre Dame is famous throughout the world, was again kindled.

Six young men after witnessing the display

of Notre Dame spirit decided to travel 3,000 miles in the fall to enroll at that famous centre of learning. Others are arranging to come for the January term. Before long a host of the future leaders of Mexican life and culture will be bringing back to their great country the loyalty to the Church and the love of learning which Notre Dame always inspires in her sons.

Good Will Ambassadors

In recognition of their distinguished services and with a view of enabling them to tie more close ly the missionary zeal of the Notre Dame students in Mexico into the Catholic Youth work, Fr. Castiello and Paul Murray were elected honorary members of the Notre Dame Club of Mexico. Thus they will be in a position to harness the enthusiasm, knowledge and zeal of all the Notre Dame men of the Republic in their glorious crusade to make Christ and His teaching reign supreme in the minds and hearts of all the people of our sister republic south of the Rio Grande.

In recognition of their notable work in promoting closer cultural and commercial relations with the United States, Mr. Harry Wright and Mr. Eduardo Mestre were likewise elected honorary members of the Notre Dame Alumni Club.

"I am glad," said Mr. Edward Trueblood, Secretary at the American Embassy, "to see you organize a Notre Dame Alumni Club here because every student, Mexican or American, educated at Notre Dame University will be a good-will ambassador, interpreting to the people of Mexico the ideals of freedom and democracy for which the United States is pouring out her blood and her treasure in all the countries of the world today."

Chapter IX
COYOACAN AND A PEON'S HOME

There is a great shortage of priests in Mexico. This is traceable to the expulsion by Calles of priests of Spanish birth, to the exile of great numbers of the native priests, and to the closing of all the seminaries in Mexico during both the Calles and the Cardenas regimes.

For a month I assisted the Franciscan Fathers at Coyoacan in bringing Mass to the people of the large territory in which they minister. It afforded me an opportunity of gaining an insight into the devotion of the Mexican people and also to become well acquainted with that historic community.

Coyoacan was an Indian community even before the days of the Aztecs. It became the first Spanish settlement near the capital. It was from here that Cortes directed the last siege of Mexico City. The present Municipal Palace is the first edifice he built immediately after the Conquest. In Coyoacan the wife of Cortes was found strangled to death, according to gossip by his own hands because he became annoyed by her jealousy. It was here too that Cuauthemoc, the last of the Aztec Princes, was tortured by the Spanish to compel him to reveal the hiding place of Montezuma's treasure.

San Juan Bautista

In front of the main plaza stands the parish church of San Juan Bautista dating from 1583. Near it is the monastery dating from 1530. Although it has undergone many changes, the church is still a splendid example of early Franciscan architecture, showing strong Aztec influence in its stone-carved decorations.

It is a common sight to see a Mexican woman setting up her little charcoal stove and cooking tortillas at the church door to sell to those who come out. There is scarcely any gathering place of Mexicans where one will not spy the inevitable tortillas being cooked and sold as they come off the burning coals. What the hamburger is in America, the tortilla is in Mexico—and more.

One morning after saying Mass, I came out the main door of the Church. I noticed a number of bullet holes in the thick wooden doors.

The Red Shirts

"These," said Fr. Ortiz, O.F.M., "are reminders of the bullets fired by the Red Shirts at the people coming out of the church one Sunday morning. It was during the Cardenas regime. The Red Shirts were avowed Communists and were holding a meeting in the plaza.

"As the doors opened at the end of Mass and the people started coming out, suddenly and without warning the Red Shirts fired point blank into the midst of the crowd, killing several and wounding others. It was not possible to bring the murderers to trial because they had the protection of government officials."

The above is but one instance of what the Church had to endure during the years of persecution. It brought one's mind back to the days of the Roman persecutions and made one wonder how such a thing could happen in the twentieth century with all its boasted enlightenment and freedom of conscience.

Four Centuries Old

It was interesting to walk out into the enclosures in the monastery. Here was a little garden in which the lay brothers were growing vegetables. Here was a little court in which chickens were cackling. Back in the rear yard were hogs. It was some-

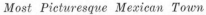

Most Picturesque Mexican Town

What is generally considered to be the most picturesque town in all Mexico is Taxco in the State of Guerrero. It is an ancient mining town founded by Borda in the seventeenth century. Its narrow winding streets and gayly painted, red-roofed houses sprawling over the hillside give the locality an unusually colorful and picturesque setting. The crown of all of Taxco's beauty is the magnificent Cathedral of Santa Prisca rising high up on the summit. It is the mecca of artists.

thing of a relic of the old days when the monastery was self-sustaining—raising all the food needed for its members. The walls enclosing the rear yard were crumbling from the wear and tear of the four centuries which weighed upon them.

While I was saying Mass at Coyoacan, the Forty Hours' Devotion was held. It was inspiring to see the faithful—men, women and children—marching around the church singing Eucharistic hymns, and approaching the Communion railing in great numbers.

Father Manuel Iglesias, O.F.M. from Rome, was making his visitation of the Order in Mexico and was staying at the monastery at that time. He is a scholar, and a man of great asceticism and holiness of life. He has the simplicity characteristic of all the sons of St. Francis of Assisi. While I was there, he received word of his appointment as Superior of the Franciscan Order in South America. Like the true soldier of Christ, he was preparing to take his brown habit, his Breviary and his holy Bible and leave for his distant post of duty in Peru.

"Blessed Poverty"

O Blessed Poverty! No packing of trunks and bags; no stewing over all the gadgets, trivia, and impedimenta which burden the citizen of this world. He had given up all for Christ and he was able to experience the truth of Christ's promise: "For my yoke is sweet and my burden is light."

On a number of Sundays I celebrated Mass for the Franciscan Fathers at one of their numerous outmissions—at Churubusco. A couple hundred natives would be on hand. As every Mexican family has at least one dog, and as they are inclined to follow their masters, the church always had a few dogs roaming in the aisles. This did not distract the simple natives nor appear to them unusual.

Returning from Mass one week-day morning at

Churubusco, I stopped to watch a man plowing a couple of acres. The plow was a primitive, hand-guided one, which kept coming out of the ground. I commented on his trouble. *"Poco a poco,"* he replied. "Little by little," he would get it plowed.

A Peon's Home

Nearby was the typical one room house in which the Mexican peon family lives. Outside was a hog tied with a rope around its neck—a common sight. Noticing my interest, a woman emerged with four little pigs in her arms to show me. On the other side of the house was a hen, tied with a six-foot string to a stick driven in the ground. A dozen little chicks were scratching around her.

"Why keep her tied?" I asked.

"To keep her out of the vegetable garden," she replied.

Two skinny dogs were lying in the sun.

I wondered what the inside of their little home was like. I had not long to wonder. The lady invited me in.

The floor was the mother earth. There was a single bed with no springs, but with a mat covering. On it was perched a hen. In a little wooden bird cage, evidently home-made, was a chick about five days old. On the wall was a picture of Our Lady of Guadalupe and on a little altar before it burned a candle. A small bouquet of flowers rested on the altar. Over in a corner was a blanket which the other members of the family apparently used for a bed. Lying on the floor were four cadaverous, mongrel dogs.

Scene within the cloistered garden of the old Franciscan Monastery at Churubusco. Note the mosaic reproduction of the famous picture of Our Lady of Guadalupe, the favorite picture of all Mexicans.

"Lost Five Children"

"Why so many dogs?" I queried.

"To watch the house," she answered.

"But they must take a lot of food," I said.

She shrugged her shoulders.

"How many in your family?"

"Two girls, one seventeen," she said, pointing to a girl working in the garden, "the other, eleven, is at school."

"I lost five children," she continued, "most of them dying in infancy."

Here she touched upon one of the poignant tragedies of Mexico—the lack of elementary knowledge of hygiene among the peasantry. In consequence it has an alarming infant mortality—126 per 1,000 as compared with 46 for the United States, according to the reports for the year 1940.

Extreme Poverty

I have visited many homes of the natives, living in the mountains and the valleys, and have been appalled at the extreme poverty under which they live. Many of the homes are adobe huts of one room, dirt floor, no bed, with a little hole in the ground serving as the place for their cooking.

As there is neither stove nor chimney, the smoke has no place to go but in the room. Ordinarily it is not so thick, however, as the fuel used is largely charcoal. But it reminds one considerably of the primitive conditions which the early Jesuit missionaries found in the wigwams of the Redskins of North America.

The inevitable altar speaks eloquently of the

deep faith of these simple people. Enduring hardships which would make us quail, they hold fast to that holy Catholic faith which has given them hope and spiritual comfort. If the government of Mexico will apply the great principles of social justice proclaimed by the Roman Pontiffs, they will do more to usher in a new day for the peons and peasantry than all the high-sounding programs of the politicians.

Chapter X
PUEBLA: "CITY OF THE ANGELS"

An interesting trip from Mexico City is to
Puebla. The road circles and climbs to a height of
11,000 feet above sea level. Winding through pine
forests, it affords a magnificent view of the snow
covered volcanoes, "Popo" and the "Sleeping
Woman."

The road passes through Huejotzingo, an Aztec
name signifying "In the Knot-grass." We stopped
to visit the lovely shaded Plaza, where hundreds
were busily displaying their market wares for sale
to the peons who had come from near and far. It
was an interesting scene, with Indians of every
description rubbing shoulders with us as we saunter-
ed among the sellers of vegetables, flowers, clothing
of vivid hues, and the inevitable tortillas.

Not far from the Plaza we visited the sixteenth
century Franciscan monastery. The church has
great carved doors, mural paintings in black and
white of the first twelve Franciscan missionaries to
Mexico. The walls are sturdy and strong, and be-
speak the thoroughness with which the early Spaniards built their Houses of God to stand through the
storms of the centuries.

Haunt Of Bandits

In Colonial days the stage-coach passed
through this settlement, which became a favorite
hunting ground for bandits. Mounted on fleet
horses, they would swoop down from the mountains
upon the stage-coach, robbing the passengers, steal-
ing the "king's silver" and then disappearing into

their mountain fortresses.

Just before Ash Wednesday, the annual Hue-jotzingo carnival seeks to recapture the glamor of an episode centering around one of the most famous and at the same time beloved of the bandits of those early days, Augustin Lorenzo. Thousands of Indians assemble in fantastic uniforms, forming battalions representing Spanish, French, Mexican and Indian soldiers, and give chase to Augustin Lorenzo and his fellow bandits.

The latter not only steal the king's silver, but also the beautiful daughter of a rich ranch owner. The soldiers ultimately capture Lorenzo but not until he has married his beautiful captive. The peace and quiet of the sleepy Indian town are banished for several days by the shooting and yelling, the music and dancing of the natives.

"City Of The Angels"

Skirting the ancient holy city of the Toltecs, Cholula, with its numerous churches, we reach Puebla de los Angeles, now shortened to Puebla. This ancient and beautiful colonial city was founded by the Spaniards on the eve of the feast of the Arch-angel St. Michael in 1531, hence "of the Angels." It is the fourth largest city of the Republic with a population of about 125,000.

About 7,000 feet above sea level, it reposes on a plain guarded by the snow-capped volcanoes. Popo-catepetl and Ixtaccihuatl on the west, Orizaba on the east, and Malintzin on the north. The architecture of Puebla is strongly influenced by Andalucian and Mudejar. The towers and domes of the churches as well as those of many public buildings and private residences are adorned with polychrome tile.

In fact the city is the centre of the Mexican Talavera pottery and tile industry, and is famous throughout the Republic for its fine products in these lines.

The soft light of the moon was falling upon the magnificent Cathedral, making it loom up as a mighty sentinel, keeping its age old vigil over the human scene below. How calm and silent it looked to me that night! It seemed to rival in its massive bulk and silent peace the snow-capped mountain peaks which surrounded it. God's great temple of peace it was, bringing its message of serenity to a feverish world.

Had Tasted Exile

I was the guest of Archbishop Vera, a holy man with the simplicity of a Franciscan. He had known exile for Christ's sake, and suffering was no stranger to him. He presented me with a copy of the diary which he had kept when in exile in the United States and which tells of his longings and his anxious solicitude for the flock to whom he could no longer minister save by the ministry of prayer. Far from making him haughty with the air of Caesar, the purple and the ermine prompted him to strive more earnestly for the humility and meekness of Him Who had not whereon to lay His head.

I said Mass in the Cathedral and drank in the beauty of its main altar, its handsomely carved chair, its Flemish tapestries designed by Rubens and presented to the Cathedral by Charles V. The paintings depicting the Way of the Cross are from the brush of the great Zapotecan Indian artist, Miguel Cabrera.

From a tower above the Archbishop's Palace, I secured a magnificent panorama of the city and of

One of the most picturesque street scenes in all Mexico is that of De Tepetates in the city of Cuernavaca. The street treminates at the entrance of a church with two tall trees framing the entrance, making it look like a picture from an artist's book. Cuernavaca is only about an hour's ride from the Capital and has churches and homes of great beauty.

the surrounding countryside. The tiled domes and
cupolas shining in their varied hues in the sun
against the background of the snow-capped volcanoes and clear skies were an unforgettable sight.
From this point of vantage one could better appreciate the large number of churches and oratories
that rose like frozen prayers above the house tops
of the city.

A Colorful Panorama

One could discern the old Jesuit church, known
as La Compania and their college now taken over
by the State. At one time it was a throbbing center of Catholic culture. Now it is made a vehicle
of the ideology of the State, with a decidedly pinkish tinge of late years.

There before me was the great Church of San
Francisco dating from 1667, with a graceful tower
and unusual Churrigueresque carvings in stone on
the facade. In this church is to be seen one of the
first holy images brought over by Cortes and his
men, a tiny figure of *Nuestra Senora de los Remedios,* with an infant in her arms. Because Cortes
carried it in all his battles, it came to be called
La Conquistadora.

Out from the city a few miles loomed up the
ancient forts of Guadalupe and Loreto, where the
Mexicans conquered the French on the fifth of
May, 1867. On the fifth of May the Indians of
Puebla reenact this victory. It is from this victory
that the name Cinco de Mayo—the fifth of May—
so popular as a name for streets, is derived.

Church And Labor

It was at the Templo de la Compania that I
met the great organizer of laborers and the cham-

pion of their rights, Father Mendez Medina Alfredo, S.J. Because of his pioneering work in the fostering of labor unions and in defending their interests, he might well be called the Father John A. Ryan of Mexico.

"Why doesn't the Church in Mexico organize the workers into Catholic guilds to protect their rights and the rights of the Church as well?" I asked.

"We try to form such organizations," he replied, "but the Calles and Cardenas regimes have rendered any large scale organizations along Catholic lines impossible.

"They want to exclude the influence of the Church from the labor movement, so that they and their henchmen can dominate it completely.

"Pretending that they have the interests of the workers at heart, they villify the Church and indoctrinate the workers with the virus of communism and anti-clericalism. While charging the Church with indifference to the workers, they deliberately prevent us from organizing guilds even of our own Catholic laborers. Therein is evidenced their unfairness and dishonesty."

Lombardo Toledano

The result of this policy over a number of years is that the largest federation of labor unions in Mexico is under the leadership of an avowed communist and bitter anti-clerical, Lombardo Toledano. He is one of the chief opponents of the Church's efforts to secure freedom to launch her far-reaching program of social justice, education and charity. He is a thorn in the side of the present enlightened and fair-minded President Camacho and undoubtedly is one of the potent influences in preventing him from restoring to the Church the freedom of action which she so sorely needs to fulfill her many sided ministry to the people of Mexico.

It is heart-breaking to see the labor movement captured with government help by the handful of communists who are using it for their own political aggrandizement and economic enrichment. Heart-breaking it is to see the Church excluded from the field which is so distinctively her own—the championship of the rights of labor and of the underprivileged.

The alienation of the masses of workers from the Church is one of the tragic results of the government shackling to which she has been so long subjected. When those shackles fall from her wrists, a new day of prosperity for the workers, of justice for the employers, and of peace, progress and enlightenment will dawn for all of the people of our sister Republic, south of the Rio Grande.

Chapter XI
TEZIUTLAN: OFF THE BEATEN PATH

There is a witchery which Puebla, "the City of the Angels," exercises upon a visitor. I had been under its spell for several days, drinking in the beauty of its great Cathedral and the loveliness of the surrounding countryside, before I was able to summon courage enough to bid my host, Archbishop Vera, a reluctant "Good-bye."

It was time, I told myself, to move on. This time I decided to go off the beaten track, to penetrate into a part of the mountain country where a tourist is seldom seen. About a hundred miles away was Teziutlan where Bishop Nicolas Corona of Papantla had established his Provisional See. A brother of my colleague, Professor Jose Corona of Notre Dame, the Bishop had graciously invited me to visit him.

He warned me, however, that the town was far off the beaten path, and that I would have to take a chance on the bus getting through. It was the rainy season, and beyond Perote there was only a dirt road which at that time of the year was usually converted into quagmires.

Indian Country

I found the Bishop's warning fully justified. Beyond Perote, our bus groaned in turmoil as it struggled axle-deep in mud. Would we make it? At times it seemed that the bus would never extricate itself from the mud's embrace. But patience and the sturdy American-made motor finally won.

I was now in Indian country and the only persons we saw from now on were Indian men, women and children walking along the road. The men usually were carrying burdens on their backs, while the women not infrequently were carrying baskets on their heads. Even the children were usually carrying something. I marveled at their Stoic endurance, for they never seemed to tire.

I said we were now in Indian country. By this I mean that as far as one could see, the inhabitants were apparently either pure Indians or overwhelmingly of Indian blood. I do not use the term *Indian* disparagingly when speaking of Mexico as essentially an Indian country. Nor do I disparage the culture or the role played by the whites in the making of Mexico.

Indian Bulks Large

I mention this explicitly because I have found that an occasional Mexican reader reacts to this term as though it were uncomplimentary. Such is, however, not the case. The Indian constitutes the broad base of the population of the nation and no one can understand Mexico who loses sight of the fact that it is essentially an Indian country with a veneer of white civilization in the towns and cities. It is the Indian folkways, crafts, arts and customs which give to the Republic much of its color and much of its distinctive appeal.

While no exact statistics are available, careful estimates indicate that about 20 percent of Mexicans are pure Indian; 55 percent *mestizo*—mixtures of white and Indian, 15 percent white. This would indicate that at least 85 percent are Indian, predominantly Indian or part Indian.

According to the census of 1930, about 14 percent of all Mexicans speak an Indian language, and approximately half of these speak no Spanish. Among the pure-blooded Indians, the Aztecs bulk the largest, numbering about 650,000. They inhabit the central plateau. Their ancestors were in control of most of Mexico when the Spaniards arrived.

Next come the Mayas, numbering about 400,-000. Their proud civilization reached its peak in the sixth century, and many are the monuments, which recent excavations have revealed, bearing witness to the industry, art and culture of this tribe. They still constitute the majority of the population of the Yucatan peninsula.

In the highlands of Oaxaca live the Zapotecs, numbering about 350,000. Along the Gulf Coast around Vera Cruz are some 75,000 Totanacs. Around Lake Patzcuaro in Michoacan dwell some 40,000 Tarascans. There are many other Indian tribes with their own languages and dialects. These are to be found especially in the more isolated mountainous country, where the natives have held on with greater tenacity to their tribal dress, customs and languages.

Mr. Harry Wright of Mexico City has had trained observers living among these tribes, making records of their spoken languages and taking movies of their distinctive customs and ceremonies. He is making available to the general public a wealth of information about these interesting Indian tribes, which was in danger of passing beyond recall.

Teziutlan Appears

These were the reflections which passed through

Bishop Nicolas Corona of Papantla, Mexico, Provisional See in Teziutlan, was driven into exile in the United States during the persecution of Calles. On returning, he had but four priests to minister to the needs of hundreds of thousands of Catholics. He now has about forty priests. It was his influence with President Camacho which has helped greatly to secure for the Church a larger measure of freedom. Many of the faithful in Bishop Corona's diocese are Mexican Indians who venerate their bishop as their spiritual father.

my mind as I looked out at the mountainous countryside and saw here and there only a cluster of
Indian huts. Patches of garden could be seen on
mountain sides and down in the valleys. We encountered no autos on this stretch of our journey, only
an occasional burro plodding patiently along with
its Indian master.

At last after some six hours of struggling, we
came within sight of Teziutlan. A sprawling town of
some 15,000, it nestles among the mountains and is
shrouded in mist most of the year. The setting sun
was shooting its departing rays across the mountains, gilding their summits with a radiance which
contrasted sharply with the shadows lengthening on
the valleys. Splotches of gold, crimson and purple
were weaving an irridescent tapestry in the sky—
the day's last burst of glory before night's sombre
pall was to wrap the countryside in darkness and
in silence.

When the bus ended its groaning journey in
the plaza before the Cathedral, I was glad to alight.
Awaiting me were the Bishop's niece and her husband. They drove me down a rough cobblestone
street that made me wonder if the rocky road
to Dublin could be any rockier. Before reaching the
Bishop's home, the cobblestones ended, and just
before turning into the Bishop's courtway, our car
bogged down in the mud and only after much ma-
neuvering did we extricate ourselves.

Bishop Corona

Waiting to greet me were Bishop Corona and
his household. "Welcome to the hospitality of Quinta
San Francisco," he said, referring to the name of
his home.

"You are a brave man to risk a journey on these roads during the rainy season," he continued. "I'm glad that you made it."

The Bishop's residence was a rambling structure situated on the mountain side overlooking a lovely valley.

Living with the Bishop were his secretary, Fr. Jose Cabezas and four seminarians in various stages of advancement toward the priesthood. The Bishop and Father Cabezas are guiding them in their studies. The arrangement is similar to that which prevailed in the early centuries, when the Bishop prepared candidates for the holy priesthood in his own home. Seminaries, as we have them today, came into being only after the Council of Trent in the sixteenth century.

Distinguished Service

The Bishop has a long record of distinguished service to Mexico and to the Church. A priest of the Congregation of the Oratory in Mexico City, he responded to the urgent plea of the Bishop of Vera Cruz and accepted the pastorate in Orizaba. He became Vicar General of Vera Cruz diocese and then, upon the establishment of the See of Papantla, was consecrated its first Bishop in February, 1923.

Driven into exile in the United States by the persecution of Calles, the Bishop returned after several years to find only four priests left in his diocese. Through tireless labor he has lifted that number to about forty. This is far too few for the hundreds of thousands of his flock, which is scattered far and wide over the mountainous countryside in the States of Puebla and Vera Cruz.

Full of zeal for his people, who for the most part are poor Indians, the Bishop has established schools, convents, and hospitals where Sisters of the Precious Blood and Sisters of the Visitation spend themselves in ministering to the bodies, minds and souls of these people and their children. Late each afternoon he goes up to the Cathedral to be a father confessor to his spiritual children. The humblest Indian can come to him, without ceremony or formality, to tell him his troubles and to receive his advice, encouragement and help.

In Footsteps Of Christ

As I watched him, seated in his confessional chair, with ragged, bare-foot Indians kneeling at his side, I thought of the gentle Christ walking over the dusty roadsides of Judea and Galilee, healing the sick, cleansing the leper, forgiving the woman guilty of adultery, washing the feet of His disciples. I seemed to hear Him say: "Learn of me, for I am meek and humble of heart." Walking in the footsteps of His divine Master, Bishop Corona is carrying to his Indian children the true meaning of Christ's Gospel in which love, humility, and service constitute a diadem of pearls. As I knelt before the altar, waiting for the father confessor to finish his labor of love, I found my heart burning within me, as it burned within the disciples as they walked with the Master on the way to Emmaus.

Rain was beating its soft tatoo upon the window panes. The side door opened intermittently. Pelted in from the rain, would come an Indian, water dripping from his serape. Laying his burden down, he would come over to kneel at the side of his shepherd to receive spiritual refreshment and

an interior warmth which would more than counter-
act the physical cold.   It was a moving picture. As
my eyes had strayed from the crucifix, so my mind
wandered, I fear, from my prayers.

"My Mind Wandered . . . "

I was thinking now how faithfully Bishop Corona, with head bowed, listening to his poor peni-
tents, symbolized the true attitude of the Church
to the Indians from the time that the first Franciscan missionary landed on the shores of New
Spain. I thought of Fray Juan de Zumarraga, the
first Bishop of Mexico in 1527, protesting to the
Emperor, Charles V, against the enslavement of the
Indians.

Though surrounded by spies, the Bishop carried
his letter to Vera Cruz, sealed it in a cake of wax
and entrusted it to a friendly sailor bound for
Spain. "If it is true," he fearlessly wrote his sov-
ereign, "that your Majesty has granted permission
to make slaves of the Indians, you should, out of
reverence to God, do humble penance." Thus did he
brave the wrath of a king to make Christ's law of
justice, mercy and love, a reality to the untutored
Redmen of the forest.

I thought of Fray Pedro de Gante organizing
his school at Texcoco and enrolling a thousand Indian children, and protecting their fathers against
the *Conquistadores* who would enslave them. No
wonder a prominent street in the capital bears his
venerated name.

I thought of Father Bartolome de las Casas
carrying his fight for the Indians to the Court of
Castile and persuading Charles V in 1542 to prom-
ulgate the Laws of the Indians.   No wonder the

people of Mexico erected his statue alongside of the Cathedral in the capital and inscribed affectionately thereon the title, "Father of the Indians." Here was the authentic mirroring of the mind of Christ and of the love of His Church for the Indian people. For the defense of the Redman, the true priest of Christ, like His divine Master, would gladly lay down his life.

"So Much For So Little"

"How much does it cost Your Excellency to maintain a seminarian for a year?" I asked as we went back through the drizzling rain to the Bishop's home.

"Living expenses are low here," he said, "and our mode of living is simple. Forty dollars would suffice."

I was astonished. That would just about maintain a seminarian for a month in our country. Here, I reflected, is a chance for people to do so much for so little.

"We are still far short of priests," said the Bishop. "We have a convent of perpetual adoration, but the sisters are without a chaplain. Are you too tired from traveling to say Holy Mass for them?"

At the altar of this convent where daughters from the finest homes in the land busied themselves in ceaseless prayer for the priests and people of Mexico, I offered the Eucharistic Sacrifice each morning during my sojourn in Teziutlan.

"All the blessings which have come to my people," said the Bishop, "I attribute to the unceasing supplications of these holy nuns."

The Light That Faileth Not

The blessings came not only to that diocese, but to all the people of Mexico. For Bishop Corona was privileged by Almighty God to bring back the mother of President Camacho to the Church, and to win the friendship, esteem and veneration of the Chief Executive and of his family. Because of his close friendship with the President, Bishop Corona is chiefly responsible for securing for the Church the large measure of freedom which she now enjoys. But that is a story to be detailed later.

I looked out that night from my room in Quinta San Francisco upon the sleeping city. On an elevation overlooking the city was the beautiful little chapel of Our Lady of Mount Carmel. A noble piece of Spanish architecture which stood on that pinnacle for more than two centuries. Lights were burning from its steeple—lights in the form of a cross. The rest of the countryside was in darkness. The setting was picturesque beyond description. That cross was blazing in the skies of Mexico the same message, I thought, which it blazed to the Emperor Constantine in the fourth century—"In this sign, thou shalt conquer." For that is the Cross invincible, and that is the Light which shall not fail.

Chapter XII
A TREK AMONG THE INDIANS

The home of Bishop Corona in Teziutlan is uniquely situated. The front gate opens on one of the main streets of the city, even though its pavement is fully as bumpy as the rocky road to Dublin. The rear gate, if there were one, would open upon the untrammelled beauty of the countryside.

Standing in his beautiful garden, with trellised vines running along the footpaths, I looked out over the sloping hillside into a green valley through which a limpid mountain stream was purling. Across the broad and fertile valley rose up a mountain upon whose side I could make out the huts of Indians. A mighty expanse of foliage, pine, spruce, maple and elm, stretched out as far as the eye could reach.

Standing atop the mountain peak, a white chapel, dwarfed by the distance, glistened under the morning sun. It stood as a perfect illustration of the fine habit of the natives in crowning their most picturesque sites with a votive chapel or shrine. How often had I gazed in rapture at such spectacles of intriguing beauty as I traveled through the countryside. How often had I found myself breathing the wish: "Oh, if I could only take that little chapel and transport it with its picturesque setting to my country, what a thrill of joy I would give so many of my countrymen."

Like Frozen Dreams

Many of them have been standing there for centuries, looking like dream castles and reflecting too the frozen dreams and prayers of the native Indians. Gazing upon the loveliness of mountain, stream, meadow and color-splashed sky, these simple people sought to mirror in their stout walled churches the beauty which they saw in nature.

I thought of the Church of the Virgen de los Remedios atop the tallest pyramid at Cholula. I thought of the Chapel of Our Lady of Mount Carmel on a hill in Teziutlan, and of the unrivalled picturesqueness of Santa Prisca rising up out of the mountainside at Taxco. Symbol of the wedding of beauty and virtue, they sounded their paeans of praise to the God of beauty, and whispered an invitation to the passerby to lift his thoughts to the things of Heaven.

"What is the name of that little chapel gleaming off there on the mountain peak?" I asked the seminarian, José, standing at my side.

"That is *La Capilla de la Montana,*" he answered. "It is a votice chapel whither the Indians working and hunting in the mountains go to pray."

"A few Sundays ago," he continued, "the coadjutor Archbishop Marquez of Puebla celebrated Mass there. Indians came from far and near. It was a gala day for them."

"Any Old Clothes?"

That white chapel was beckoning and calling me—challenging me to climb to its lofty portal.

"Have you any old clothes that I could borrow?" I inquired.

"Sure. I'll fix you up. We'll need old clothes too because we'll most likely be caught in the rain before we can get back. For that is a day's trip."

Attired in old clothes, with a huge Mexican sombrero shading my eyes from the sun, I set out with José into the wilderness of valley and mountain where no tourist had ever set foot.

Pushing our way through shrubbery and bushes, we finally reached the stream rippling through the bottom of the valley. But here the undergrowth was so thick we could not see our objective nor find any trail leading in that direction. At last we

Many a landscape is given a background of grandeur and beauty by the great snowcapped volcano, Popocatepetl, which dominates so much of the Mexican countryside.

came upon an Indian carrying his inevitable pack on his back and obtained his assistance.

With the courtesy so characteristic of these people, he cheerfully laid down his burden and guided us through the underbrush to a trail leading to the mountainside.

We climbed for several hours. Then we came upon a little cluster of Indian huts.

It was a good chance to get a rest and to have another visit inside one of these homes. I could not get over their primitiveness and the absence of almost everything we in America have come to regard as necessary for the comfort of a home.

Inside An Indian Home

I knocked at the door. An Indian woman opened it and eyed me with interest and with some wonderment in her face. Apparently I was as curious a spectacle to her as she and her abode were to me.

"He's a *padre*," said José, "and wonders if he might go in for a little and rest."

Instantly her face brightened, and a smile crept over her features.

"You're welcome indeed, Father," she said. "Come in."

The room was almost bare. The earth was the floor. Over in the corner was a primitive cot. The woman had some maize and resumed her interrupted work of grinding it on a stone. Not a book or newspaper, nor lamp in the house.

Here was poverty the like of which is virtually unknown in America.

"I don't see the usual charcoal fire," I said.

"Oh, we have that in the other room."

She lead us into it, and there was a girl of about 10, busy kindling the fire. She was shy and inclined to retreat behind her mother's skirts.

The house was superior to that of many, if not to most, of the huts of the Indian peasants in that they had a second room in which to do their cooking and thus kept the smoke from the room in which they lived. In most of the Indian huts I had entered, the cooking was done in the one and only room of the house, and the smoke was not pleasant to the eyes.

"Where is your husband?" I inquired.

"He's working on the hard road the President is building into Teziutlan."

Our Lady's Picture

We went back into the living room and there in the semi-darkness I perceived a picture of Our Lady of Guadalupe with a little branch from a pine tree in a vase before it.

I marvelled again, as I had so many times before, at the almost invariable presence of a picture of Our Lady or of Our Savior. The faith of these people remains unaffected by government edict. So deep had the early Spanish missionaries planted it, that it seemed now to be an integral and inescapable part of them.

I gave her and her little child my blessing and we departed.

Our next stop was at a Church half way up the mountainside. It was an outmission, where Mass was celebrated, because of the shortage of priests, only a few times a year. It was neat and clean and we lingered some time in prayer before the main altar—praying for the welfare of the Mexican people who have experienced so many vicissitudes of revolution and religious persecution.

As we came out of the Church an elderly Indian who turned out to be the caretaker of the Church came up to us. Upon learning that I was a

priest, he insisted upon guiding us up the footpaths that led to the summit.

After another hour of climbing we reached
the peak. I was surprised to find a half dozen
Indians standing along the side of the chapel. On
talking to them we found they were all in a tipsy
condition.

An Indian, with his bundle of pottery, taking a brief
rest. Mexican Indians carry enormous bundles on their
backs, and quickly put up shop at any corner.

It was pitiable to think that to all their hardships and deprivations they would voluntarily add
the vice of intemperance. I was sorry to learn later
that the demon of rum was already spreading his
blight upon many of these natives, thus chaining
them more securely to their prison of poverty and
want.

We entered the little chapel. The floor was
strewn with branches of pine. The altar was neat

and clean.   Here again we bowed our heads in
prayer.

An Inspiring Vista

Outside the view was inspiring.   One could see
for many miles in all directions.   Little Indian huts
were perched on every mountain side and in the
valley.   Scratched patches of earth around their
huts told of their means of livelihood.   Poor in
this world's goods, they were rich with the beauty
of nature round about them.   The mountain peak
stretched like a pointed finger of prayer to heaven,
while the setting sun splashed crimson and gold
with lavish hand upon the canvas of the sky.   Rain
was beginning to fall and soon the irridescent colors
of the rainbow were encircling us, transforming our
mountain into a fairyland of beauty and fantasy.

It was difficult to leave our summit, with inspiring vistas stretching out in every direction, but
soon darkness would fall and our descent would be
more difficult.   So after one last lingering view we
bade farewell to one of the most beautiful and
picturesque views we had in all Mexico—the more
enjoyable because it was nature almost untouched
by man and his industrial civilization.

The trek down was rendered somewhat hazard-
ous by the rain which made the paths slippery.   In
spite of the help of the Indian guide who had at-
tached himself to my side, I slipped a few times
and found myself embracing mother earth.   The
consciousness that I was wearing old clothes, however, lessened my discomfiture.

"Padrecito"

Imagine our surprise when upon nearing the
church half way down the mountain, we saw a

crowd of Indians awaiting us. One of their number was ringing the Church bell with great vigor. Word that a priest was among them spread rapidly from hut to hut and here they were, waiting to welcome me and to lead me into their church. "Padrecito," the affectionate term for "Father," was on the lips of the men, women and children as they sought my hand.

How my heart went out to them, as they stood there in the drenching rain, so eager to welcome a priest of God. They knew something of the Calvary through which the priests of Mexico had passed and they were anxious to demonstrate their affection for the ambassadors of God.

We went into the Church and prayed together, reciting the Rosary. Then I said a few simple words to them.

"Hold fast," I said, "to the faith of Jesus Christ, the faith planted among you by the saintly missionaries from Spain. Though poor in this world's goods, you possess the priceless treasure of the faith of Christ. You are members of that great family which numbers its children by the hundreds of millions and unites you with your co-religionists in every land."

This was the theme I developed briefly. They listened with rapt attention and some nodded their heads to express agreement. I gave them all my blessing. Many of them accompanied us a mile or so down the mountain side to be sure we would find our way. They are a kind, gracious and courteous people and they won both my esteem and my affection.

I should add that my appearance in secular garb was neither new nor irregular to them. For many years the wearing of clerical garb has been prohibited by the anti-religious statutes. It is a common sight to see a Franciscan with tan shoes and a Jesuit with a soft collar and colored tie—and bishops as well.

A Welcome Sight

The sprawling city of Teziutlan was a welcome sight that night to two tired travelers. We were drenched to the skin, and had been without food since breakfast.

As we descended the rocky road to the Bishop's house, a man was walking on unsteady legs before us. At any moment he appeared as though he would terminate his journey by falling prostrate to the ground. At last he did.

A dog ran out and wagging its tail, sought to rouse him and lead him to his home nearby. It was a touching scene. In spite of his master's disgraceful condition, he was still his faithful friend, standing by him when even his friends would be ashamed of him. I thought of the words of Byron, inscribed over his own Newfoundland:

But the poor dog, in life the firmest friend,

The first to welcome, foremost to defend.

Here again was the tell-tale evidence of the blight that liquor was spreading among these people, as it has among so many. When, I wondered, will humanity wipe this plague from their midst?

The lights were already shining from the spire of the Church of Mt. Carmel when we reached the gate that led from the noise of the city to the quiet of the Bishop's garden—a little isthmus between the city and the untouched beauty of the valley and the mountain. Late though we were, José and I were still in time for the 9 o'clock evening meal so common in Mexico.   It had been a long and strenuous day but full of the simple joy of tramping out-of-doors and drinking in the beauty of the mountain landscape and feeling the warm impact of the *sympatia* of the Indians of Mexico.

Chapter XIII

ACAPULCO—THE PEARL OF THE PACIFIC

The visitor to Mexico, who sojourns for several months in the Capital, eventually experiences the urge to push on to Acapulco, the oldest and most beautiful seaport on the Pacific coast. The charm of its bathing beaches and the lure of its modern hotels are proclaimed throughout the Republic. The chilly afternoon rains and the cold nights in Mexico City whetted our appetites for a good swim and a touch of the tropical sunshine.

The trip to Acapulco by auto is a good twelve hours run. It can be made by plane in an hour. We set out in our car over the road that runs through Cuernavaca and Tasco.

Out from Tasco the road winds through valley and mountain in a region of gorgeous scenery. This area is rich in ore. Back in the days of the Aztecs, gold was extracted from the Guerrero mines. It is believed today that Indians know of hidden veins of the precious metal.

The road leads into Chilpancingo, now called C. Bravo, the quaint old capital of the State of Guerrero. It lies in a fertile well watered region with an abundance of flowers and vegetation. We paused for refreshments in the plaza, where an Indian woman proferred us the inevitable tortillas. The drive through the mountain air had given an edge to our appetites, and we banished for the time being any scruples about hygienic cooking and devoured the tortillas.

Discovered By Cortes

Continuing our journey, we passed through Mazatlan, Palo Blanco with its beautiful landscape, Acahuizotla with its tropical vegetation and came at last to Acapulco. The name dates from the Aztecs and means "Place of Reeds." It has a population of about 8,000. It was discovered by Cortes

Acapulco, Mexico's Tropical Paradise

Caleta beach in Acapulco, or "Morning" beach, as it is sometimes called, is thronged with happy bathers unable to resist the lure of the water.

in 1513 and became an important port in the trade between Spain and the Philippines. Silks, spices, ceramics and jewels arrived in merchant ships and were carried in a three-week march to Vera Cruz to be sent thence to the Old World. Later the bay served as a refuge for the harried merchant ships scurrying from the buccaneers. Almost every type of ancient vessel, slave ships, merchantmen, galiots and whalers, dropped anchor behind its protecting bluffs. It was here that Hernando de Alarcon outfitted his expedition for the voyage that was to lead him to the discovery of California. It was from this port that the great Mexican missionary, San Felipe de Jesus, sailed on his voyage to Japan to win the crown of martyrdom. The ancient Castle of San Diego, which surrendered in August, 1913, to Gen. D. José Maria Morelos, is still standing, scarred with the ravages of time.

The bay is about four miles long and two wide, and is enclosed by mountains. The beach is excellent and we had several good swims there, though the huge breakers pushed us before them with little difficulty. It was invigorating to struggle about in the salty water and have the waves break over our heads, making us feel so tiny and so helpless in the grip of the mighty sea.

We took a sail boat for a ride of a few hours and witnessed the native in charge catch a half dozen large turtles. When one would come up to bask in the sun the sailor would steer his vessel quietly close by, and hurl a spear into the shell and pull the victim aboard. They can be had by the passengers for the asking and are cooked and served in the restaurants to suit the tastes of the

owners.   One of them made a delicious meal for
us that evening.

Romance And Magic

Visitors will find it worthwhile to visit Roqueta
Island, the Quebrada, Pie de la Cuesta and Laguna
de Tres Palos, which afford inspiring vistas of the
waters of the Pacific shimmering in the rays of
the sun. The view from Pie de la Cuesta, a point
jutting out from the rocks, is especially memorable.
On one side mighty breakers were spending their
fury on the white sand. On the other, a peaceful
lagoon was lapping gently at the feet of a steaming
jungle. Something of the romance and magic of
Tahiti hovered over this spot.

Up on the cliffs are a number of modern hotels
rivalling those of the United States and of Europe
in the beauty of their appointment. They enjoy a
picturesque setting and afford a lovely view of the
Pacific. Those down on the beach, likewise offer
all reasonable comforts.

We strolled through the quaint old town and
paused in the market place. Natives were selling
pottery, ornaments made of sea shells, gold chains
and earrings fashioned by local goldsmiths. We
could not help but notice that among the natives
were many negroes who spoke Spanish with fluency.
There seemed to exist no color line and all mingled
together as members of a large family.

Facing the plaza stands the principal Church of
the town. We entered and knelt in prayer before
the Blessed Sacrament. Around this altar, I reflected, the natives of Acapulco find peace and a
quiet joy which surpasses even the happiness which
comes from viewing the sunlit waters of the Pacific

or swimming amidst its foam crested breakers. For there in the tabernacle is the Source of all beauty Who alone can give peace in its fullness to the restless hearts of men.

Acapulco's market is filled with colors, sweet scents, and people. Women dodge traffic with bundles balanced easily on their heads.

Chapter XIV
VERACRUZ: TOWN OF THE HOLY CROSS

Veracruz is the chief seaport along the Eastern coast. It was so named by Cortés because he landed there on Good Friday, 1519, and called it *La Villa de la Veracruz,* meaning "The Rich Town of the Holy Cross." Here was established the first Spanish settlement. It now boasts of a population of about 75,000 and its docks are the scene of much activity when the merchant ships plying along the Gulf unload their cargoes.

We journeyed down from the Capital in an over-night train from Mexico City. Accustomed as we were to the cool climate of the Capital, we felt keenly the tropical heat with the thermometer hovring around 100 degrees. The city presents a picturesque combination of the old and the new, with modern office buildings contrasting with gaily painted wooden houses, extending porches, palms and flowering trees.

The Plaza with an arcade restaurant twining around it, offers the traveler an interesting place to relax. All types of people were passing in and out. Men, women and children beseiged us to sell us lottery tickets—but all to no avail. I could not help reflecting upon the much greater fruitfulness which would accrue to the nation if the vast army of lottery ticket venders were put to constructive service. One sees them, barefooted and often in rags, at all hours of the day and night, shouting their wares, as they waste their time and energy in this, the most useless of all occupations.

Memories of Other Days

The Cathedral loomed up before us, with many worshippers coming in and out. It brought to my mind my first visit to Veracruz in the summer of 1936. It was during the Cardenas regime when the anti-religious group was still in the saddle. The Governor of the State of Veracruz, the notorious Victor Manero, had outdone the federal government in his persecution of the Church, refusing to license a single priest to minister to the religious needs of the people.

Bishop Guizar y Valencia, one of the saints among the hierarchy of Mexico, was in hiding in Mexico City. It was a vivid tale of continuous and relentless suppression of all the activity of the Church which the good bishop narrated to me. A house in which a priest celebrated Mass, would, if the act were discovered, be confiscated and a reward given to the informer. The priests took to the mountains, and disguised as peasants continued to minister to their scattered flocks and at night time to bring the sacraments to the sick and the dying in the city of Veracruz.

When I met the bishop, he was wearing an old suit that even a hobo might have disdained. Needless to say there were no pectoral Cross and no Roman collar.

"Where in the world, bishop, did you get that suit?" I asked.

"From the city hospital, where the owner of it recently died," he replied.

Mexican Catacombs

His pectoral cross he had sold to buy food for some of his starving flock. He walked among the poor and lowly of his flock as one of them and ministered to them with the charity of Christ. His priests and people loved him and would have died for him. But the bishop wanted no bloodshed, and forbade them to resort to violence. It would have meant the futile loss of life against the well armed soldiery.

Upon learning that I was to go to Veracruz, the bishop delegated unusual faculties to me to assist in keeping alive the ministry of religion among the flock from whom he was exiled.

What memories came back to me! I had hunt-

The Patio of the Convent of San Agustin Acolman

Just off the Highway Laredo-Mexico City at Km. 100, you pass the village of Actopan with its handsome Agustinian church and convent. The convent has fine frescoes in black and white. The native specialties are handwoven bags and sashes.

ed all Sunday morning, the day I arrived, to find a
priest in hiding so that I might say Mass, as all the
churches were closed.   After some four hours of
searching, I finally found one.   He was wearing a
white suit, seeking to throw any suspicious persons
off the trail.   He escorted me to an orphanage on
the outskirts of the city, where nuns cared for
orphans from very poor families.   It was so poverty
stricken that the *politicos* had not sought to confis-
cate it.

There at 12 o'clock, I offered up the Holy Sac-

The Convent of Actopan

Nearing Mexico City at Km. 34 a road turns to the
left, leading to the pyramids of Teotihuacan and the convent of San Agustin Acolman.   The convent was started
in 1539 and is a strong handsome structure, with fine
Mexican Plateresque decorations over the entrance.   It
also has magnificent murals and a beautiful patio with
well preserved frescoes.

rifice in the presence of about 8 nuns and 60 orphans. A table was used as an altar and the window shades were carefully drawn for fear that
any prying eye might detect what was taking place
and cause trouble. It was like saying Mass in the
Catacombs during the Roman persecutions.

That long nightmare for the Church has now,
thank God, happily passed. The churches are once
more open to admit worshippers to exercise the
elementary right of citizens of every free country
in the civilized world—the right of worshipping
God according to the dictates of their conscience.
The enlightened regime of President Camacho has
refused to countenance the persecution of the
Church which had become the pet sport and the
chief source of income for the anticlerical politicians.

Cordoba and Orizaba

Out in the bay ships were pulling into the harbor with buzzards flying around them. There is a
bathing beach, but good bathing is not one of the
attractions, and the person who has enjoyed the
beach and the clean waters at Acapulco will find
little inclination to swim here.

We took a ride on a steam launch around the
harbor, stopping at the Castle of San Juan de Ulua,
built in 1528 to mark the spot where Juan de Grijalva first landed. It is now used as a military
prison.

It is well to return to Mexico City by the day
train to take in the gorgeous scenery. The train
climbs to a height of 7,500 feet, and passes through
tropical meadows, crosses bridges, and stops at
quaint villages where Indians bring gardenias and

other tropical flowers and fruits to sell to the passengers.

We stopped for a while at Cordoba and at Orizaba, picturesque cities with populations of 18,000 and 45,000. The view afforded of the three snow-capped volcanoes, Pico de Orizaba, Popocatepetl and Ixtaccihuatl, the "Sleeping Woman," is indeed inspiring. The tallest of these is Orizaba, being 18,225 foot high and the most difficult to climb.

Late that evening we arrived in Mexico City, and the faster tempo of life combined with the kindly face of the venerable Cathedral, looking down upon the earthly pilgrims below, made us feel like arriving home.

Chapter XV
A PANORAMA OF MEXICAN ART

The visitor interested in popular art will find in Mexico a variety and an artistic quality unsurpassed in any country on the American continent and in few other countries. Since the majority of the people is living in an agricultural, handicraft civilization, they produce practically everything they need at home. They are not content, however, to turn out plain simple things but embellish them with pictures of flowers, birds, plants and animals. Into their textiles they weave fish, birds, plants and flowers. It is difficult to find a piece of leather which is not covered with elaborate figures and tracings.

The mosaics of colored straw are the finest that I have seen anywhere in the world. Especially exquisite are the mosaics executed by F. Ariza. Two of them adorn my mantlepiece and visitors find them objects of never ending wonderment and delight. Since time means nothing to most of these people, they cheerfully devote long periods of labor to minute details in mosaic, textile and wood carving which would stagger the average American workman.

The Mexicans are the descendants of a race of artists and sculptors whose work is being increasingly dug out of the buried past by archeological expeditions. The country is a great storehouse of archeological treasures, some interesting specimens of which are on exhibition at the *Museo Nacional* in the capital.

Outstanding among these is the Aztec Calendar Stone, an immense basalt carved disk, with the sun in the middle and around the edges the twenty signs of the days of the month. It is thought to have been used also as a sacrificial stone, dedicated to the sun god. The Aztecs and Mayas are said to have had astronomically correct calendars before the Europeans.

Archeological Treasures

On the second floor of the Museum there is the famous Monte Alban Exhibition. This is said to represent the greatest archeological treasure ever discovered on the American Continent, in Tomb 7, Monte Alban. The discovery was made by Alfonso Caso, archeologist and the director of the Museum.

Archeologists tell us that the Indian tribes first settled in the north of the country with a gradual migration to the south. The languages and characteristic mental traits of these tribes were most varied. Two however, became outstanding and dominated the others in many ways. First was the Mayas who spread from the Gulf of Mexico and the territory now constituting the State of Chiapas to Central America. They were the more civilized and were chiefly responsible for the progress achieved in the arts and the sciences. Relics of their civilization are encountered along the Gulf of Mexico, in the States of Tamaulipas, Veracruz and Tabasco. Then the trail follows along the course of the great rivers Grijalva and Usumacinta, and continues in Chiapas and in the south of Campeche to Yucatan which is especially rich in archeological treasures.

The second group which rose to great power

was the Nahoas, hunters and warriors famed for their conquests. When these came in contact with the Mayas, the civilization of the Maya triumphed over the physical prowess of the Nahaos, giving rise to a new civilization, the Tolteca, which extended from its origin in the center of Mexico to all the other ethnological groups.

Relics of their civilization stretch out in all directions from their great city, Teotihuacan, to

The Palace of Fine Art in Mexico City is one of the most impressive buildings in the Republic and houses some of the nation's most treasured paintings.

Zacatecas, to Morelos, to Oaxaca with its great Monte Alban treasure. Through the southeast stretches a trail of their monuments running down into Yucatan where they modified the monuments originally constructed by the Mayas to whom they owed their first knowledge of architecture.

Modern Art Movement

There is a modern art movement in Mexico of much promise. The institution which was the cradle of Mexican art and has been its nursery for a century and a half is the National School of Fine Arts. Formerly called the Academy of San Carlos, it was founded by Charles III in 1791 and has been the most important institution of its kind in the Country. In its galleries hang one of the most valuable collections of painting in the Republic and perhaps in the entire American continent.

Here are assembled the works of the best of the Mexican Colonial painters: Sebastian Ortoga, José Ibarra, Miguel Cabrera, Baltasar de Echave, the brothers Juarez, José Albizar, Carlos de Villapando as well as the work of the best of the modern group. There are likewise many fine paintings brought from Europe to hang in the churches during the Colonial period. These are included among the paintings as a result of the Reform Laws, nationalizing ecclesiastical property. Since 1934, many of these paintings have been removed to the Palace of Fine Arts where they can now be seen.

The leaders of the modern art movement are José Clemente Orozco and Diego Rivera. Among the younger men of promise are Rufino Tamayo, Carlos Mérida, David Alfaro Siqueiros, Julio Castellanos and Carlos Orozco Romero.

I had an interesting visit with Federico Mariscal, one of the architects of the *Palacio de Bellas Artes*. As a professor of art in the National University, and as a productive artist himself, Mr. Mariscal is exercising a fine influence upon the development of Mexican Art, both in painting and in sculpturing.

Satires In Wood

In one of my many visits to the *Palacio de Bellas Artes,* I viewed an exhibit of wood carvings by Carlos Basanez Rocha of Jalapa, in the state of Veracruz. For the most part they are caricatures, satires in wood. On first view they gave the impression of almost unrelieved ugliness. The more I studied the figures and deciphered the thought of the sculptor, the more they gave me a sense of great power and unusual capacity for invective. Instead of seeking to please the eye with mere prettiness of form, the sculptor sought to grip the mind with a thought, and an arresting thought at that. The longer I tarried before his sculptured satires, the more I felt that beneath the ugliness of shape and figure was the power of an idea that scorned the approval of the mere senses and strove for the deeper approbation of the mind.

Outstanding among his sculptures was the figure, A Concept of Justice. Mr. Rocha is a lawyer by profession, and apparently had some experiences which convinced him that what is sometimes passed out as justice may be but a grotesque mockery. The figure is ugly, and at first glance the spectator is likely to shy away from it. But if he stands his ground and studies the detail, I think he can scarcely fail to be impressed with the articulate hideousness of the figure.

Noticing the care with which I was studying the sinister figure, a man approached me to inquire my reaction. He proved to be the sculptor himself. He then told me how he had come to represent the

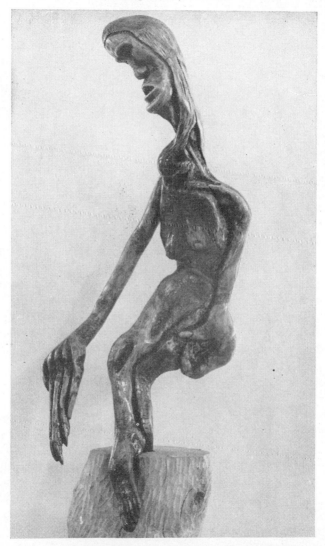

A satire in wood by the lawyer sculptor, Carlos Basanez Rocha of Jalapa. Note the crookedness of every member of the body seeking to depict the dishonesty of the ostensible dispenser of justice.

noble virtue by so ugly a figure instead of by the
usual pleasing female. He had seen cases in his
work as a lawyer where bribery, corruption, power,
privilege, wrote the verdict instead of the facts and
the principles of law. He determined to represent
this caricature of justice by a crooked figure, crooked in every line of her body, with the long covetous
fingers of one hand stretched out for all that could
be reached, and with the left hand clutching close
to her side the secret bribe.

A Growing Contribution

So impressd was I with the power of the representation, that I sent out, with the sculptor's permission, to the School of Fine Arts to secure an
expert photographer to try to capture in black and
white something of the sinister power of the sculpture. As I recalled instance after instance of the
looting of churches, schools, monasteries and even
of the homes of religious people, and the inability
of the owners to make the dishonest *politicos* dis-
gorge, or to secure from the courts any redress of
their grievances, I could see the unique aptness of
Rocha's crooked and ugly figure.

What a splendid hobby this was. Mr. Rocha
made no claims for formal artistic training. He
had ideas and he found an enormous delight in
struggling for long hours in seeking to compel the
hard wood to mirror these ideas. All this work he
did in his leisure time. What a lesson it is to most
of us to use our leisure in a hobby which challenges
our power of expression and develops a faculty
which is not called upon in our ordinary avocation.

In the Palace of Fine Arts on opposite walls
are large frescoes by Orozco and Rivera. The for-

mer depicts the chaos of our present day world and is done with a lustiness of color and a flaming revolutionary spirit. Rivera's fresco is designed to portray Man at the Crossroads, and embodies the painter's uncritical glorification of the communism of Lenin and Trotsky. It is of inferior artistic quality.

There are on exhibition many other paintings which I found of greater interest and appeal. The paintings in the Palacio will not equal those of the Louvre in Paris, the Pitti Palace in Florence, nor the Museum of Art in New York, but they are noble works and will repay many a visit. They reflect the age-old hunger of man to reflect his vision of beauty of color, symmetry of figure, grace of outline, his eternal effort to freeze into lasting marble something of the transient splendor of setting suns and to imprison upon the canvas colors that were never seen before on land or sea. Mexico is now making a valuable contribution to the many patterned tapestry of the world's art and culture and that contribution is destined to grow in significance with the coming years.

Chapter XVI

A CHURCH FOR AMERICAN CATHOLICS

The Catholic tourist from the United States who sojourns in the capital for any considerable time will be interested in knowing that a church has been designated as the parish church for the English speaking people. It is the church of *Nuestra Senora de la Paz*, 7 Enrico Martinez St., of which the Rev. Euardo de la Peza, S.J., is the pastor. It is centrally located and at one of the Masses the sermon is preached in English. Confessions in English are likewise heard.

I had several pleasant visits at the home of Father de la Peza who has lived in the United States for a number of years and was ordained to the holy priesthood by the late Cardinal Gibbons of Baltimore. Familiar with American life and customs, Father de la Peza is likewise a deep student of Mexican affairs and is in a unique position to give helpful suggestions and guidance to American Catholic visitors interested in getting a true insight into the religious conditions of Mexico.

Americans who plan to move their families to Mexico will find his guidance helpful. Likewise tourists who have been misled by misinformed or prejudiced guides will find from this learned and kindly Jesuit the truth concerning the history of the Church in Mexico and the problems confronting her today.

In assisting at his Mass on Sunday morning, I was happy to discover that two of the leading men of his parish, Guillermo Colin and Carlos Barousse

were old students of mine a quarter of a century ago
at the University of Illinois.   It brought back old
memories to me and made me feel very much at
home.   Mr. Colin has become one of the leading
organic chemists of the Republic, and Mr. Barousse,
one of its gifted architects.   They and their families,
—they both married Illinois girls—Josephine Twigg
and Helen Toohey, constitute the nucleus of the
University of Illinois Club which I founded in
Mexico City in the summer of 1936.

Americans who attend the summer session of
the National University of Mexico are usually giv-
en solely the government side in the Church-State
controversy which raged for many years up until
the enlightened regime of President Camacho.   I
listened to Mr. Ramon Beteta present the viewpoint
of the Cardenas regime, picturing one side all black
and the other side all white. It would be a great contribution to the cause of truth and enlightenment if
the University would bring scholars like Father de
la Peza, Father Alfonso Castiello, S.J., Professor
Albert Maria Carreno and Father Mariano Cuevas,
S.J., the most eminent historian of the Church in
Mexico, to present in a dispassionate manner the
objective evidence upon which alone a correct judg-
ment on a controversial issue can be formed.

While visiting in the down-town district, Catholics will appreciate the privilege of making a visit
to their Eucharistic Lord in the Church of San
Felipe, where Exposition of the Blessed Sacrament
is held from early morning till nine o'clock in the
evening every day of the year.   Located on Avenida
Francisco I. Madero, across from Sanborns where
all Americans go both for food and drugs, this

beautiful church will afford the Catholic visitor an opportunity to pray and meditate and to refresh himself with the spiritual strength that will keep him wholesome and good, and enable him to get the most out of his sojourn in the country whose civilization was planted four centuries ago by the missionaries from Spain.

Chapter XVII
SYNARCHISM: THE HOPE OF MEXICO

During the administration of Lazaro Cardenas, the powerful machinery of the federal government was thrown into high gear to pull Mexico away from its ancient moorings and establish a Communist regime. The political, social, economic and atheistic ideology of Karl Marx received a veneration scarcely second to that given to it in Moscow. Diego Rivera and José Clemente Orozco painted its message of class strife, of hatred for property owners, and scorn for religion in lurid colors on the walls of the *Palacio de Bellas Artes,* of the National Palace, and of the National Preparatory School in the capital.

Business men and industrialists found themselves shackled with labor laws inspired by the agitator, Lombardo Toledano. He had returned from Moscow with the avowed determination to transform Mexico into the image of the Soviet State. His labor syndicates were deftly used to give the appearance of popular backing to the revolutionary measures initiated by Cardenas. Breathing hatred of property owners and scoffing at religion, Toledano and his syndicates became the spearhead of the Communist attack upon the established order.

I was in the Capital in the summer of 1936 when Toledano had called a general strike. The prominence of the Red Banner and the pictures of Lenin and Trotsky made a visitor wonder whether he was in Moscow or in Mexico.

Church In Catacombs

In some of the States only a few clergy were licensed to practice, while in others not a single one was permitted to minister. Not a single religious school was allowed to operate. The Church was driven once again into the catacombs.

Frantic efforts were made to convert the schools into agencies for the imposition of Marxian ideology upon the young. I was at a meeting of the Committee on Cultural Relations with Latin America, held in the capital in 1936, when the Secretary of Education declared publicly that it was the aim of the government to teach the doctrines of Communism in all its schools.

"There are many kinds of Communism," said an American delegate. "What kind of Communism are you endeavoring to teach and to establish in Mexico?"

Without hesitation the Secretary replied:

"The Communism of Karl Marx. We are teaching it in all schools, from the lowest to the highest."

Meaning Of Synarchism

It was this determined effort of Cardenas, Toledano, and of a small clique who were in the saddle, to tear Mexico away from her traditions, to uproot the religion of the overwhelming majority of the inarticulate masses, and to impose by governmental force the odious system of the Soviets upon the people, that brought into being the Synarchist movement.

The term, *Synarchism,* meaning *with order,* was chosen to indicate its opposition to anarchy, which means without order. While the meaning the term seeks to convey is admirable enough, the name

sounds strange and utterly meaningless to the un-
initiated. The choice is, I think, an unhappy one.
Doubly so, because it has the same *ism* ending as
the three odious names, Nazism, Fascism, Communism. I propose "Christian Democracy" as the name
which best describes the essential nature of the
movement, and the goal of all their striving. If that
name be adopted, more than half the suspicions
clustering around it will fade away.

Then too the significance of their salute has
been frequently misconstrued. The Synarchists
salute by placing their right arm across their chest
till the hand almost touches the left shoulder. This
has been interpreted as merely a diagonal variation
of the Fascist and Nazist salutes. Actually it indi-
cates the laborer is about to remove the burden from
his shoulders. It is a symbol of the emancipation
of the peasant from his role of a beast of burden.

Origin Of Movement

The National Synarchist Union was founded on
May 23, 1937, at Leon, Guanajuato, when three law-
yers, Maneul Zermeno, Jose Trueba Olivares, and
Salvador Abascal met with a farmer, Jose Antonio
Urquiza. They determined to oppose the class strife,
anarchy and persecution of religion, which the apostles of Communism had unleashed, by launching a
movement for the establishment of a Christian
Social Order.

Condemning Communism, totalitarianism, dic-
tatorships and tyrannies, repudiating divisions of
leftists and *rightists,* of *revolutionaries* and *reac-
tionaries,* the Synarchists seek to unify the people of
Mexico behind certain broad principles in harmony
with their traditions and their genius. Making it

clear that they want no Nazi swastika or Communist
star or any other foreign symbol, they stand for the
right of private property in accordance with the
natural law and with the principles of Christianity.
They condemn, however, the injustices and privileges with which it was often invested by economic
liberalism.

Seek Justice For All

In contrast to the class strife upon which the
Communists depend to achieve their revolutionary
goal, the Synarchists endeavor to promote effective
and legal cooperation between capital and labor.
They seek to translate the principles of the labor encyclicals of Popes Leo XIII and of Pius XI by securing full social justice for the workers in the factories and on the farm. They lay emphasis upon the
dignity of the human personality and upon the first
duty of capital to pay a decent living wage to all
workers. The object of their solicitude is the peon
who has been so often the victim of fraud and in-
justice.

"How are you going to achieve these laudable
ends?" I asked various leaders whom I met throughout the Republic.

"We are proceeding slowly," replied one of the
leaders in the capital. We have a National Committee directing the entire movement. Under it are
the Regional Committees which correspond roughly
to committees for the different States. These control
Municipal Committees which in turn direct the activities of Rural Sub-Committees. We believe that
the first requisite for success is the systematic organization of all classes, especially the peasants and
workers."

A Political Organization?

More than half a million members, I was informed, have been recruited. Each day brings more members, as the basic principles of the movement make a natural and spontaneous appeal to the peasants and workers who have so often been exploited by foreign companies and by the politicos within their own government.

"Is Synarchism a political movement?" I asked a leader.

"No," he replied. "We have purposely kept out of partisan politics, but we seek to cooperate in all activities which seek the general welfare of the people.

"While we do not oppose the Government," he continued, "we point out abuses of the Government. If necessary we may even offer passive resistance to arbitrary impositions contrary to the ideals and instincts of our people.

"We attend meetings in a democratic, orderly and peaceful manner. All members are unarmed, as we deprecate the use of violence from which our country has suffered so much."

A "Fifth Column"?

"There is the suspicion in some circles in Mexico and in the United States," I said to a leader of the movement in Puebla, "that your organization is influenced by Nazis, Fascists and Falangists, and that it is a form of a 'fifth column' in the service of the Axis powers."

"That is stupid slander," he replied, "spread by papers that are either misinformed or that are in sympathy with Communism.

"Notice the next time you see such an insinua-

tion," he continued, "and see if the paper carrying
that libel is not of the pinkish character. In the eyes
of some journalists in this country and in yours, any
one who stands resolutely opposed to Soviet atheism
is suspected of being unpatriotic. We love the Rus-
sian people, but we despise the atheistic Communism
which Lenin, Trotsky and Stalin have sought to
impose upon them by starving more of their own
people than the Germans have slain. We shall never
submit to dictation from the Comintern in Moscow
which is planning revolutions in your country and in
mine at the very time Russia is receiving help from
both of our countries.

Oppose Communism

"Let me quote for you and for the American
people," he continued, "what our platform has to say
about Communism: 'Synarchism is the absolute denial of atheism and of communistic irreligiousness.
It is opposed to, and the adversary of, historical
materialism; it is opposed to the delusive society
without classes; it is the struggle against class war
and class hatred. Synarchism is the defender of
private property, it is the liberator of our peasant
class, for whom it desires the private ownership of
the land; it is the liberator of our workers, for whom
it desires likewise a just distribution of property;
it is the destruction of those exploiting and rapa-
cious capitalists of the type which the revolution
has produced. Synarchism is also the destruction of
the leaders who live at the expense of the worker
they deceive and corrupt.' Synarchism combats
communism in every field and seeks to expel from
Mexico its teachings and practices."

As the Synarchist leader read to me his organi-

The "pyramid of the Sun" and the "pyramid of the Moon" have their names from and old Aztec legend, telling how all the gods gathered at Teotihuacan, when the world was in darkness, and prepared a great fire. The god Nanuatzin leaped into the flames and reappeared as the sun. Tocociztecatl would make the same, but failed to reach the glowing heart of the fire and reappeared as the moon.

The pyramid of the Sun is 66 meters high, the pyramid of the Moon 42 meters. The pyramids are divided into several pyramidal terraces and surrounded by a variety of buildings and platforms. The view from the top of the pyramid of the Sun is delightful. A tunnel reveals the inside structure, made of adobe.

Teotihuacan has an excellent auto road, by which it is reached from Mexico City in about an hour (distance 45 Km.) The road leads you past the Sanctuary of Guadalupe and many other interesting villages. On the way you can visit San Acatepec with the monument to Morelos, Tepexpam, and the Convent of Acolman. You need for the visit of the pyramids not more than half a day.

zation's vehement condemnation of Communism, an incident came to my mind. I was the guest at a luncheon arranged for me by Mr. Edward Trueblood, Secretary of the American Embassy. He had invited some of the scholars of Mexico to meet me, Professors Edmundo O'Gorman and Mariano Alcocer of the National University of Mexico, and Father Gabriel Mendez Plancarte, editor of the literary monthly, *Abside*.

"Semi-Fascists?"

"What do you think of the Synarchists?" I asked.

"Oh, they are an organization of semi-Fascists," replied Professor O'Gorman.

"May I ask why you term them *semi-Fascists?*" I inquired.

"Well, really," he answered, "I don't know much about them. Perhaps because Hitler and Mussolini condemned Communism so often and so strongly, and then turned on the democracies, we are a little inclined to suspect as Fascist any organization that now condemns Communism."

The professor was wrong, I'm convinced, in thinking of the Synarchists as semi-Fascists, but right in pointing out the origin of the tendency to apply the label so indiscriminately. Because Churchmen in South American countries have continued to denounce Communism, shallow and flippant journalists have pictured them as in sympathy with the Fascists. This, of course, is a *non-sequitur*, and represents the inability to think straight.

Does Synarchism condemn Fascism and Nazism with equal earnestness? I looked up its platform and find a statement, which translated, declares:

"Synarchism maintains that no social program could be established in Mexico upon the principles of Nazism, Fascism or any other totalitarian form of government. Totalitarianism would mean the end and destruction of all Synarchist efforts, of all its sacrifices and of all its ideals and aspirations.

"The totalitarian State repudiates the natural right; to it, the only source of right is governmental power, and this is the worst of all tyrannies, because it is tyranny which converts the law into the pretext and accomplice of its excesses. It constitutes itself the ultimate and supreme aim in such a manner that the individual's only reason for existing is his usefulness to the State, for which he should sacrifice everything, including his soul. It disposes of private property in the manner that suits it; it destroys the family by taking possession of the children; it crushes all private initiative and creates a single official party, obliging all to belong thereto. Synarchism is the emphatic, calm, definite denial of all totalitarianisms. The principles of Synarchism force it to be irreconcilable with them."

A Religious Organization?

Some journalists in this country have pictured the Synarchist Union as a religious organization, controlled at least in part by the Church. Is this true? In all my inquiries among the clergy, I never found one who was a member or who was even connected with the movement. I find its national platform thus specifically disavows being a religious movement:

"Any social program destined for Mexico should be based on the principles of the Christian and democratic life of its people. Synarchism seeks constantly to unite all Mexicans in a spirit of national unity, because this unity constitutes peace, prosperity and strength. However, Synarchism wishes all people to realize that it is not a religious movement.

"Synarchism demands that all its members be men of consistent honesty in all fields of their activities; but it does not bear the standard of a religious movement, nor does it number among its ranks a single member of the clergy.

"A social program for Mexico should recognize the great importance of the family, protecting it and promoting its growth. Family life is the foundation of civil society; it is necessary for the formation of the man and for the development of all those virtues which are an inseparable part of Christian civilization."

Education And Social Justice

Recognizing that the greatest problem of Mexico is the education of its people, Synarchism demands complete freedom of education and will not rest content until there is not a single illiterate person in the Republic. Since seventy per cent of the population lives off the land, Synarchism will center its major efforts on rural education for both children and adults.

Its platform on labor demands full social justice for the worker, declaring:

"Synarchism looks forward to the dawn of that day in which all workers shall receive just recompense; in which there shall be superior conditions of hygiene and safety; that day in which the laboring classes shall have a share in the profits of the factories; Synarchism shall try each time more to restrict the work of women and children; Synarchism will fight that the State may fulfill its proper function, that of aiding and developing industry; of protecting the weak, to the end of assuring the common good.

"But Synarchism goes further. It demands an end to class war, a cessation of those unjustified strikes which are contrary to the law and are organized with the aid of politicians and unscrupulous officials. It is indispensable that the manner of Synarchism be raised, that the strikes destructive to our incipient industry be ended. This hour, in which the country demands the coordination and subordination of private and class interests, is the hour in which Synarchism finds its greatest justification, since the President of the Republic echoes its call for a united country in this sentence of his address to the Congress on September 1, 1941: 'Neither employers nor employees should forget that they are, above all, Mexicans, and that the unity of the country comes first.'"

Pro-American Sentiment

Mr. Raleigh Gibson, secretary at the American Embassy, when informed of my intention to make an investigation of the real nature of this movement, requested me to be on the look-out to see if there were any tinge of anti-American feeling in it. I did so. After several months of investigation, I was able to report:

"Far from finding any antipathy to the United States, I find a wide-spread respect and admiration. These people are anxious to clasp our outstretched hand in genuine and enduring friendship. Naturally they wish, like all freedom loving people, to work out their own national destiny, and have no

RELIGIOUS

Is the Chur
tirely so, how n
the anti-clerical
regimes been n
churchos, sch
What is the a
ministration?

These are
millions of A
which have
came into off
public south
deal. Many
ico is accon
privileges
enjoys.

Befor
findings,
world's l
cratic n
Axis po
support
Americ
deepen
not les
the sa

uine
cordi

publics, precludes an honest effort to ascertain the true position of the Church and to state those findings in a frank, objective and friendly manner. For we believe it is a truism to say that the most effective policy for Mexico to pursue, to increase the respect and good will of her North American neighbor is to recognize and to apply the same principles of religious freedom which are part of our national heritage and of our pride as well. Whatever then is conducive to that end may well be viewed as steps in the direction of closer and more enduring ties based upon common principles of civilization and common ideals of liberty.

During the campaign for the presidency, General Almazan made a strong appeal for the suffrages of that large body of the electorate which had become thoroughly disgusted with the anti-religious policies of both Calles and Cardenas. The former aroused the antagonism of the liberty loving people of America by his brutal and bloody persecution of the Church, climaxed by his execution of the Jesuit, Father Pro, for the crime of persisting in ministering to the spiritual needs of the Mexican people. The persecution of Calles was marked by violence and bloodshed. The persecution of Cardenas was characterized by subtility and craft.

Cardenas Regime

Apparently recognizing that the blood of martyrs is the seed of Christians, Lazaro Cardenas passed up the gun and the sword for the more subtle weapons of the book and the school. His plan was to root Christianity out of the young and to instill Communism and a crude form of atheistic materialism into them. Teachers in the public schools were required to sign a renunciation of the Catholic faith, which was referred to as "fanaticismo" under penalty of losing their jobs.

A determined effort was made to capture the consciences of the little children by instilling in their young minds a hatred of the clergy as well as of all who owned property. Textbooks seething with the Marxian ideology of the class struggle and scorn for religion were prescribed not only for the public schools but for the few private schools which were allowed to operate. The crucifix, holy pictures, and all religious symbols were proscribed under penalty of closing the school. I visited a school conducted by nuns, wearing lay attire, where the Blessed Sacrament was kept hidden in a book-case, for no tabernacle or chapel was permitted.

"At any moment," said the sister, "a government inspector may suddenly come into our school. If he find a Crucifix, a rosary or even a catechism, we shall be forbidden to operate. We are living," she added, "as in the days of the catacombs."

Persecution Unpopular

The persecution of the Church was the work of a small clique of so-called liberals, of strategically placed officials and of generals who were looting the churches and growing fat on the fines arbitrarily imposed. A Masonic influence was much in evidence. The persecution was never popular, however, with the masses of the people, who were deeply Catholic in heart even if they did not actively practice their religion.

It was to this great majority of people that Almazan directed his bid for support. He promised emancipation for the Church and religious freedom for all. Vast numbers who had never voted before turned out in response to his plea to register a vote of protest against the anti-religious policy of Cardenas and a vote for a new deal for the Church and for all who owned property.

It is generally admitted that Almazan received from 70 to 85 per cent of the vote cast. The writer did not find a single person who denied that Almazan received the great majority of votes. Such, however, counts for little in Mexico. It is the president in power who controls the army and who determines the winner. Cardenas turned thumbs down on Almazan and declared General Camacho elected. Rather than risk a civil war and the wholesale shedding of blood against the overwhelming odds of the government controlled army, Almazan bade his followers to sheathe their swords while he faded out of the picture.

A Pleasant Surprise

Mexico is a land of surprises. And a surprise as pleasant as it was unexpected was in store for the long suffering Mexican people. Shortly after assuming office and getting control of the army, and placing his powerful brother Maximino, former Governor of the State of Puebla, into his cabinet, President Camacho announced a new deal. Freedom of religious worship was to become the order of the day. Declaring that he was a baptized Catholic, he affirmed that his Administration would guarantee freedom of conscience and freedom for the Church to minister to the spiritual needs of her children.

The president's mother died a practical Catholic, and her funeral service was conducted by Bishop Nicolas Corona of Teziutlan. Present besides the

President and General Maximino and his other brother, a colonel in the army, were most of the other generals. The sight of the President and all the generals at Mass was a new spectacle for the people of Mexico and seemed to augur a new day for the Church in the land of blood-drenched altars. The president's wife is a practical Catholic. The president is a nominal one at present, but it is hoped that soon he too may set an example for the men of Mexico by practicing his professed faith, and thus make his practice square with his profession.

What Caused Shift?

What caused President Camacho to shift from the Communist, Church-hating policy of Cardenas to the present, enlightened one of liberty for the Church and of reasonable consideration for the much harried property owner? We cannot say that we know all the factors.

These, however, seem sufficiently evident. There is the influence of his mother's example—for she returned to the Church after a long absence and the sincerity of her repentance and the devotion she displayed before her death undoubtedly made a deep impression upon him.

Then there was the clear evidence of the unpopularity of the Church-shackling policy of Cardenas, as registered in the majority vote for Almazan, which was essentially a vote of protest. This gave Camacho a perception of what the Mexican people really wanted.

Another factor is the growth of the Synarchist movement which now numbers more than half a million members in its organization. The Synarchists are not fascists, as superficial American

writers have reported in our secular press. They
are seeking essentially to apply the great principles
of sound justice, formulated particularly in the
Encyclicals, *Rerum Novarum* and *Quadragesimo
Anno,* to Mexican life and industry.

Opposing Communism with all their might,
they are striving for the realization of a Christian
social order, with special concern for the poor and
downtrodden and with justice for all. The consciousness of this great organization, which thus
far has wisely kept aloof from partisan politics, is
undoubtedly a source of strength and encouragement for Camacho to break away from the Soviet-
minded policy of his predecessor.

Anti-Clerical Forces

Does the Church enjoy as yet complete liberty?
No. The whole set of anti-clerical laws are still on
the statute books and could readily be enforced at
any moment. Furthermore, there are two sets of
forces restraining Camacho's evident desire to free
her entirely from her chains. The first is Lazaro
Cardenas, who is still a power behind the scenes,
and whose hatred of the Church has shown no signs
of abating. The second is Lombardo Toledano,
leader of the Labor Syndicates, avowed Communist
and notorious enemy of the Church. While in
Mexico City this summer, I heard him attack Camacho in a great open air meeting for granting too
many concessions to the Church and for thus "jeop-
ardizing the hard-won gains of the Revolutionaries."

That these two sets of forces, along with the
Masonic influence never absent in shuffling Mexico's political cards, are exercising their pull upon
the Administration's religious policy, would seem

to be evidenced by the following incident, which to my knowledge has never been published in the press of Mexico or of the United States.

In the latter part of June, arrangements were made for the staging of a great public demonstration of loyalty and of homage to the Holy Father in Commemoration of his silver jubilee, as a bishop. The *Fronton Mexico,* one of the largest halls in Mexico City, was secured. Archbishop Martinez was to climax the affair with a fifteen minute address to be broadcast throughout the nation. Congregations assembled in the Churches of Mexico to listen to the discourse.

Thus was the Church to symbolize her emergence from the catacombs into the clear light of day. It would be the first public meeting of a religious character to be staged in the Capital in many years. For great public gatherings had hitherto been held chiefly to afford Communist agitators like Toledano or other "revolucionarios" or anti-clericals to hold forth. Public gatherings for religious purposes were, however, strictly taboo.

A Crushing Disappointment

The eventful day arrived. Things began to happen fast. At three o'clock that afternoon, after all arrangements had of course been completed, the Church authorities were suddenly informed they could not use the great main hall. Only a side room, capable of accommodating a mere fraction of those wishing to attend, would be available. It was a crushing disappointment. The worst, however, was yet to come.

Fifteen minutes before the archbishop was to broadcast, word was received that under no circum-

stances was the Archbishop to be permitted to speak
over the broadcasting system! The blow was a
crushing one. Particularly in view of the fact that
the archbishop had been so generous in calling upon
his people to rally to the support of the government
in its declaration of war against the Axis, and in
many other appeals to his flock to stand loyally behind the constituted civil authorities in all their
efforts for the upbuilding of Mexico.

A Breathing Spell

Bitter indeed must have been his disappointment upon learning that his generous and unstinted
support of the government was to be repaid by ingratitude, and worse than ingratitude, stark dis-
crimination against the leading representative of
the Church which embraces more than ninety per
cent of the people of Mexico. Jazz singers can broadcast. Lombardo Toledano can broadcast. But the
archbishop of Mexico City cannot be permitted to
broadcast a word of religion or a tribute of homage
to the Vicar of Christ on earth!

The Church in Mexico is enjoying a breathing
spell of peace and liberty. We pray it may be prolonged and lengthened into complete freedom.
Candor and a decent regard for actual facts, however, compel us to acknowledge sadly that the
Church in Mexico is not as yet free from the many
chains which have so long enshackled her. We hope,
however, that President Camacho will have the courage to go all the way, and allow the Church that
freedom which we in this country regard as an inherent part of our heritage and an inherent part of
the democratic way of life for which both America
and Mexico are fighting today.

QUESTIONS FOR DISCUSSION

Chapter I

1. What is it that gives to Mexico a distinctive atmosphere and color?
2. What varieties of architecture are to be found in Mexico City?
3. The remains of what three civilizations are found throughout much of Mexico?
4. Why may the churches be said to echo memories of Spain?
5. What has become a fashion among certain modern writers on Mexico?
6. Who did the greatest work for the natives of Mexico? Why?
7. Why are so many churches at times found in a small settlement?
8. The persecution of the Church was instigated largely by whom?
9. What is the key to the understanding of Mexico? Why?
10. How may we deepen the ties of Mexico and the United States?

Chapter II

1. What form of government obtains in Mexico?
2. How many states are there in Mexico?
3. Describe the form of the government of Mexico.
4. What two great mountain ranges run through Mexico?
5. What is the population of Mexico?

6. What per cent of the blood of the nation is Indian?
7. Why is Mexico a land of striking contrast?
8. What economic class is largely missing in Mexico?
9. What is the consequence of that lack?
10. Why may Mexico be said to be largely an Indian country?

Chapter III

1. When was the International highway from Laredo to Mexico City completed?
2. Describe the scenes one encounters from the windows of a railroad coach.
3. What is the condition of many of the men, women and children selling food to passengers?
4. Describe the founding of Monterrey.
5. Who brought the first printing press to Mexico? And when?
6. Describe the city plan one finds followed consistently through Mexico.
7. Describe the city of San Luis Potosi.
8. Why is Queretaro historically important?
9. Describe the scene at the market place there.
10. What celebration takes place there on Christmas Eve?

Chapter IV

1. Describe the climate and the location of Mexico City.
2. What is its population?
3. By whom was it founded?
4. What two snow-peaked volcanos are visible from the capital?

5. Relate the legend of the Aztecs in regard to the founding of Mexico City.

6. What scene greeted the Spaniards when they first reached Mexico City?

7. Describe the setting for the Cathedral in Mexico City.

8. What historic incidents and pageants took place before the Cathedral?

9. Who rubbed shoulders in entering the Cathedral?

10. The Cathedral stands as a reminder of what great truth?

Chapter V

1. The Cathedral was erected upon the ruins of what?

2. When was the present Cathedral begun?

3. What side altar in the Cathedral attracts much attention from visitors?

4. Describe the vista from the Cathedral towers.

5. Who was the great protector of the Indians?

6. What Church is the center of Eucharistic devotion in the capital?

7. Describe the Palace of Art.

8. What two paintings are on prominent display there?

9. What are the names of their two authors?

10. What criticism of their ideology might be made?

Chapter VI

1. What is the chief shrine in Mexico?

2. How does it compare in age with Lourdes?

3. Tell of the apparition of the Virgin.

4. To whom did she appear?

5. Tell the story of the miraculous picture.
6. Tell of the Papal approval of the devotion.
7. What attempts were made to destroy the picture of Our Lady?
8. How did the faithful respond to the danger?
9. Why do pilgrims from all parts of the country come to the Shrine?

Chapter VII

1. Tell of the pyramids at San Juan Teotihuacan.
2. How do they compare in size with the pyramids in Egypt?
3. Who were the victims at these pagan sacrifices?
4. Tell of the churches at Cholula.
5. Why are there so many?
6. Why was one built on top of a pyramid there?
7. What does that church symbolize so eloquently?

Chapter VIII

1. Tell of the Catholic Action work of Miss Sofia del Valle.
2. What urgent need does it meet?
3. How many people are reached through that work?
4. How is it supported?
5. Who may be said to be the first Catholic woman of Mexico?
6. Tell of the work of Father Jaime Castiello, S.J.
7. Describe the work of Father Alfonso Castiello, S.J.
8. Why was the Notre Dame Club formed in Mexico?
9. Why may the graduates from Catholic colleges

in America now living in Mexico, be said to be ambassadors of good will?

Chapter IX

1. Why is there a great dearth of priests in Mexico?
2. Tell of the founding of Coyoacan.
3. Describe a typical scene before the door of the church at Coyoacan.
4. What incident took place in the Plaza before the church?
5. Describe the scene within the monastic enclosure.
6. Tell of Father Iglesias and his work.
7. Describe the exterior of a peon's home.
8. Describe the interior of such a home.
9. What animals are numerous in such homes?
10. Discuss the extreme poverty obtaining among such people.

Chapter X

1. Describe the scene at the Plaza at Huejotzingo.
2. In the colonial days it was the favorite haunting ground of whom?
3. What incident is redramatized?
4. Describe the city of Puebla.
5. Who is the Archbishop there?
6. Tell of his experiences.
7. Describe the panorama from the tower of the Archbishop's palace.
8. Discuss the Church and labor in Mexico.
9. Who is Lombardo Toledano?
10. What policy does he stand for?

Chapter XI

1. Who is the Bishop of Papantla? And in what city does he live?
2. Describe the journey to Teziutlan.
3. Why may the Indians be said to constitute the broad base of the population of Mexico?
4. About what percent of Mexicans are pure Indians?
5. About what percent are mestizos?
6. About what percent are thought to be pure white?
7. Describe the leading Indian tribes.
8. Describe the scene upon reaching Teziutlan.
9. Tell of the distinguished service of Bishop Corona.
10. Relate the reflections of the writer while kneeling in the Church.
11. How much does it cost to maintain a seminarian for a year in that diocese?

Chapter XII

1. Tell of the unique location of Bishop Corona's home.
2. What object in the distance challenged the writer?
3. Where have the Mexicans the habit of erecting votive chapels?
4. Describe the journey to the chapel on the mountain.
5. Describe the visit in the Indian home.
6. Whose picture was honored in that home?
7. What was the condition of the natives upon the mountain summit?
8. Describe the vista from the mountain peak.

9. Tell of the affectionate welcome of the Indians.
10. What incident occured after returning to Teziutlan?

Chapter XIII

1. How many hours by auto is Acapulco from the capital?
2. Describe the journey there.
3. By whom and when was Acapulco discovered?
4. What historic incidents are connected with that city?
5. Describe the view from the cliff overlooking the sea.

Chapter XIV

1. When did Cortez land at Vera Cruz?
2. How did the city derive its name?
3. Describe the scene at the Plaza of the city.
4. What memories of other days did it recall?
5. Who is honored as one of the saints among the Bishops of Mexico?
6. Tell of the author's difficulty in seeking to find a place to celebrate Mass.
7. Describe the city of Cordoba.

Chapter XV

1. What can you tell of the artistic traits of the natives of Mexico?
2. They are skillful in making mosaics of what?
3. Describe the Aztec Calendar Stone.
4. What archeological treasures are to be seen in the national museum?
5. What two Indian tribes were dominant in the early history of Mexico?
6. Describe the modern art movement in Mexico.

7. Who are some of the leaders of the modern art movement?
8. Describe the satires in wood.
9. Describe the figure entitled "A Concept of Justice."
10. Is Mexico making a significant contribution to modern art?

Chapter XVI

1. What is the name of the church for the English-speaking people in Mexico City?
2. Who is its pastor?
3. The Church offers a good opportunity for what?

Chapter XVII

1. During the Cardenas administration what party was favored?
2. What ideology did the government seek to teach in the schools?
3. What is the meaning of Synarchism?
4. When and by whom was it founded?
5. Why does it oppose Communism?
6. What encyclicals does it seek to translate into action.
7. How many members does Synarchism have?
8. What does Synarchism say of Fascism and Nazism?
9. What is its platform on labor?
10. Why is Synarchism a movement of great promise to the Mexican people?

Chapter XVIII

1. What impression obtains among the American people in regard to religious liberty in Mexico?
2. What was the nature of the policies of Calles and of Cardenas?
3. How did Cardenas seek to enforce his policy?
4. Why was the persecution of the Church unpopular?
5. How did President Camacho surprise the Mexican people?
6. What role did Bishop Corona play and how?
7. What influence does the Synarchist movement exercise in this matter?
8. What anticlerical forces are still functioning?
9. What was the experience of Archbishop Martinez?
10. What is its significance?

INDEX